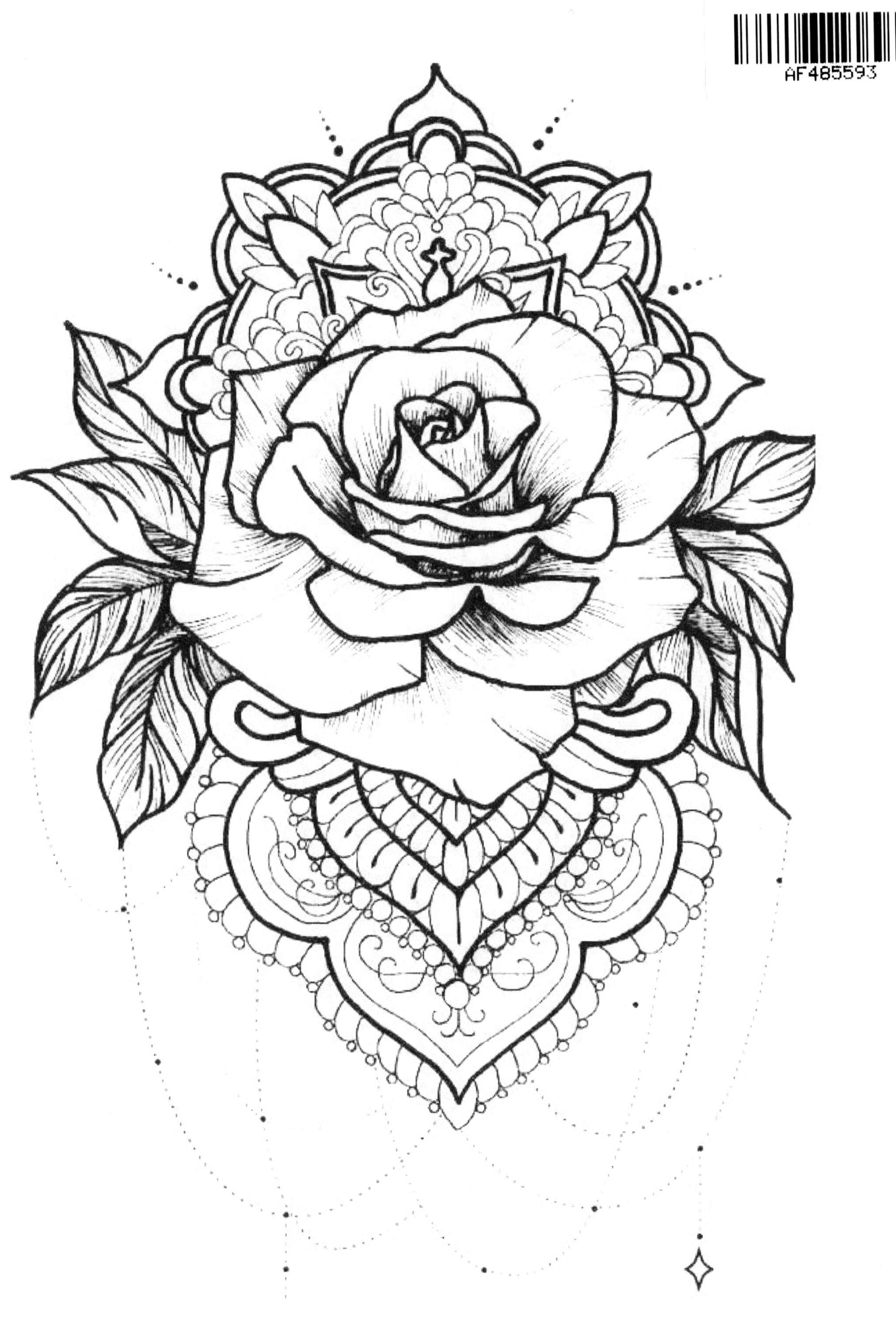

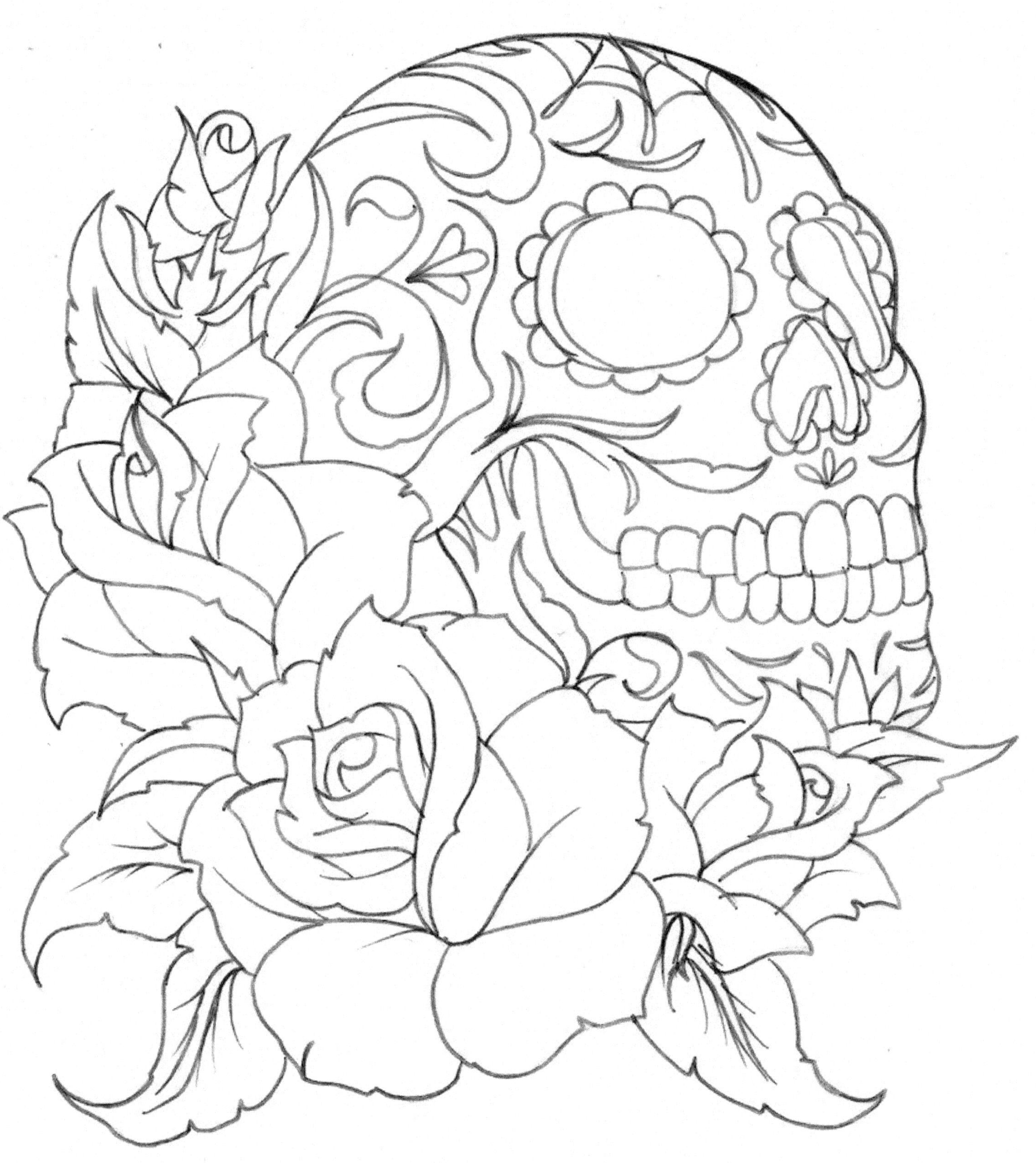

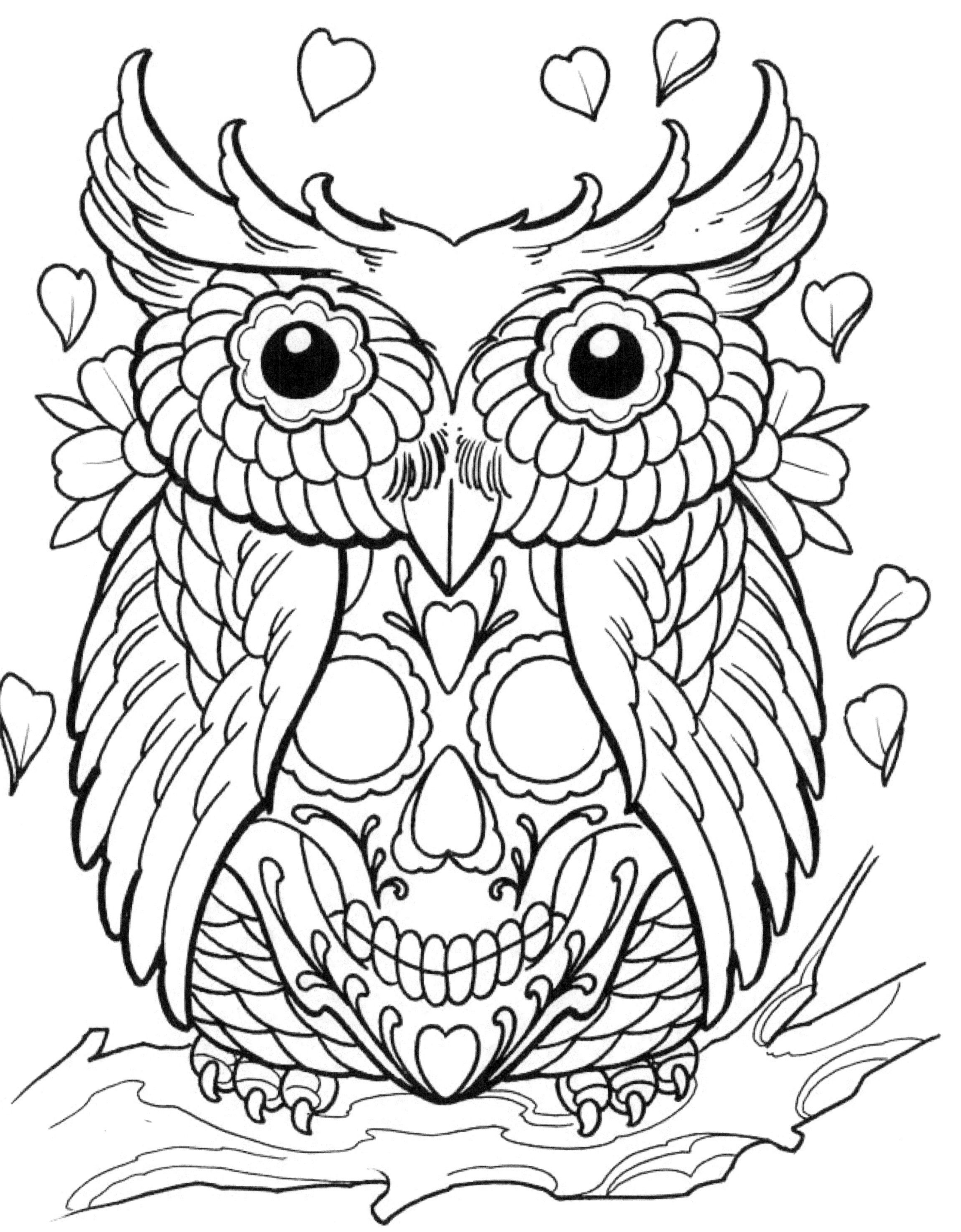

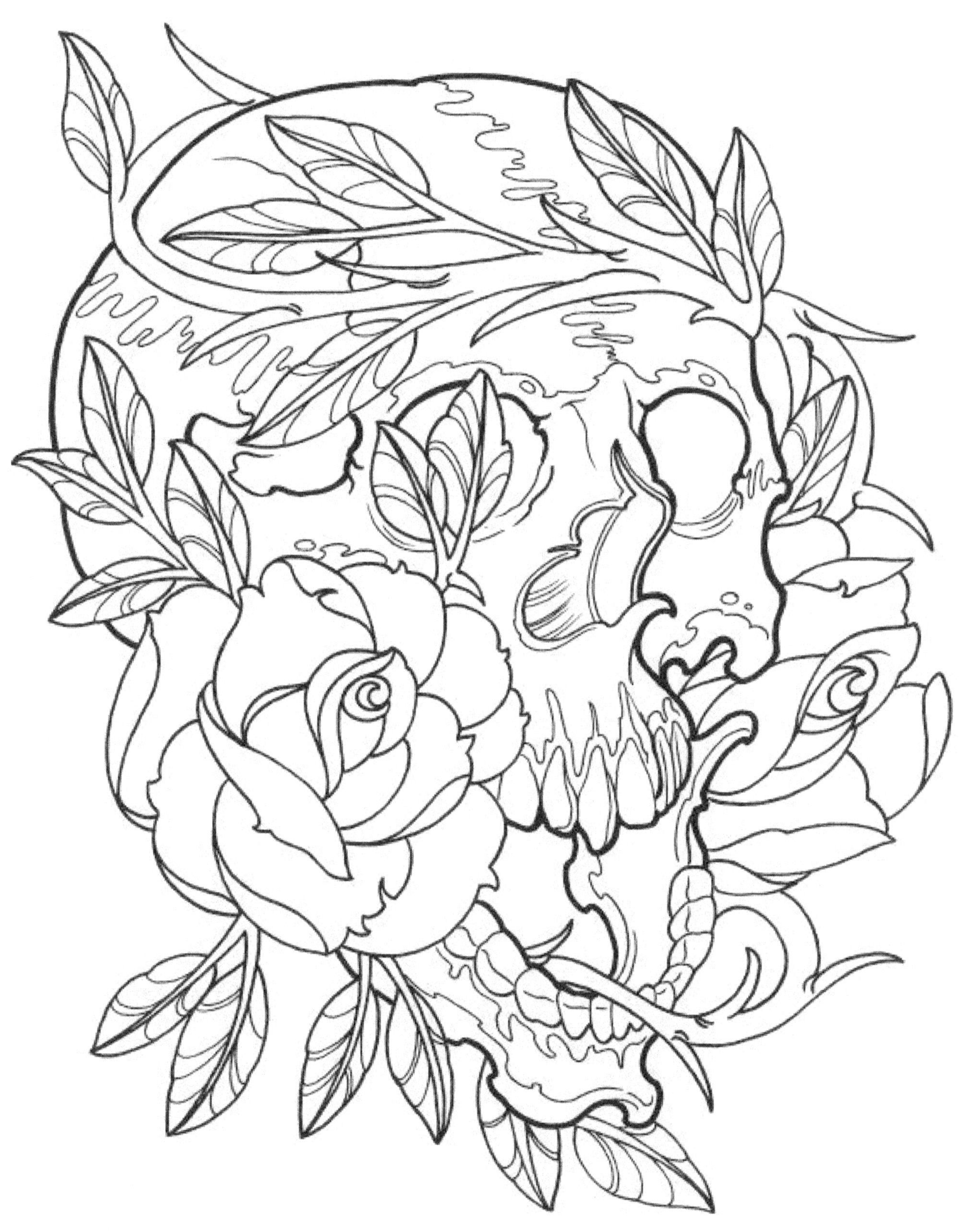

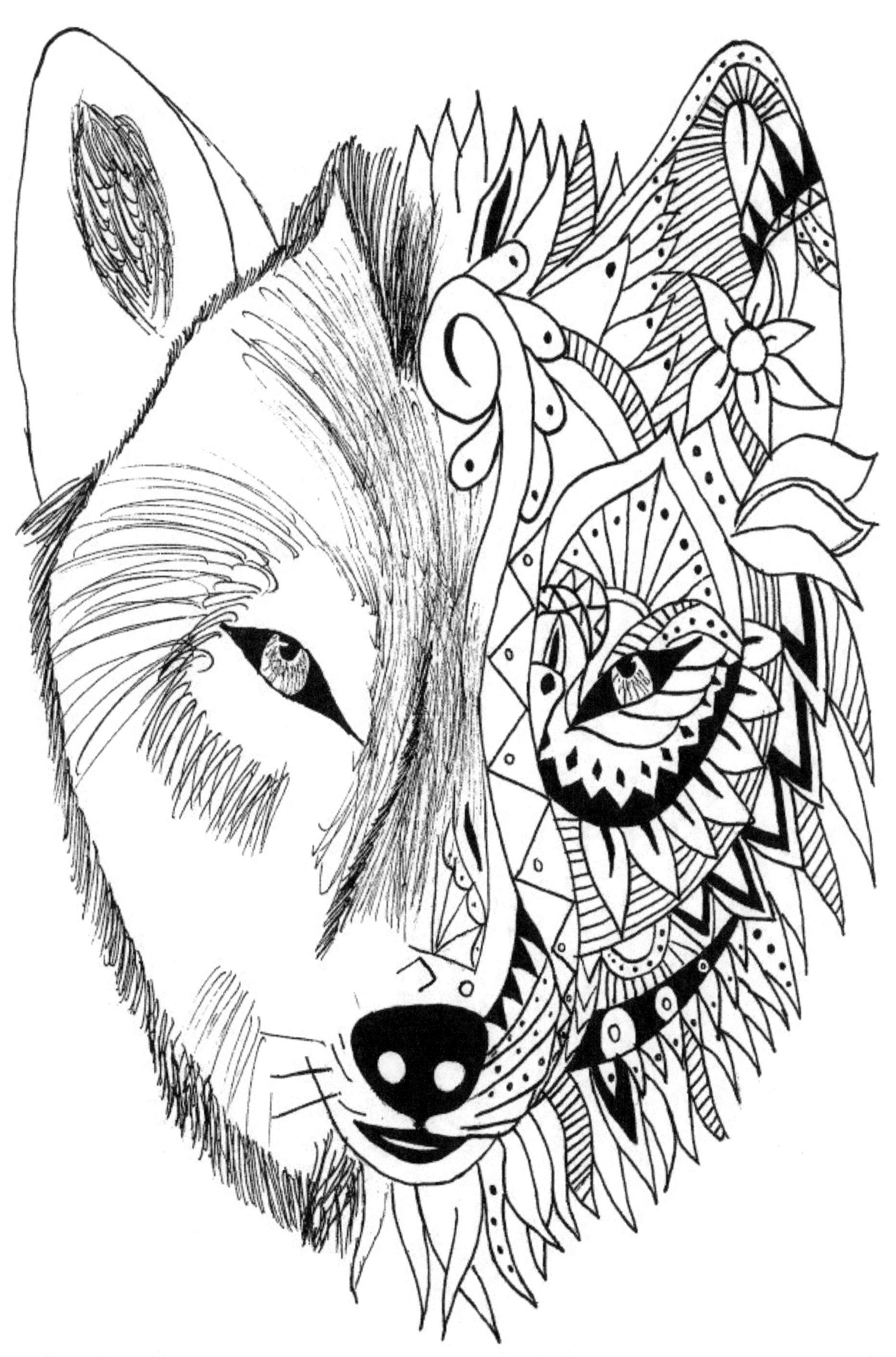

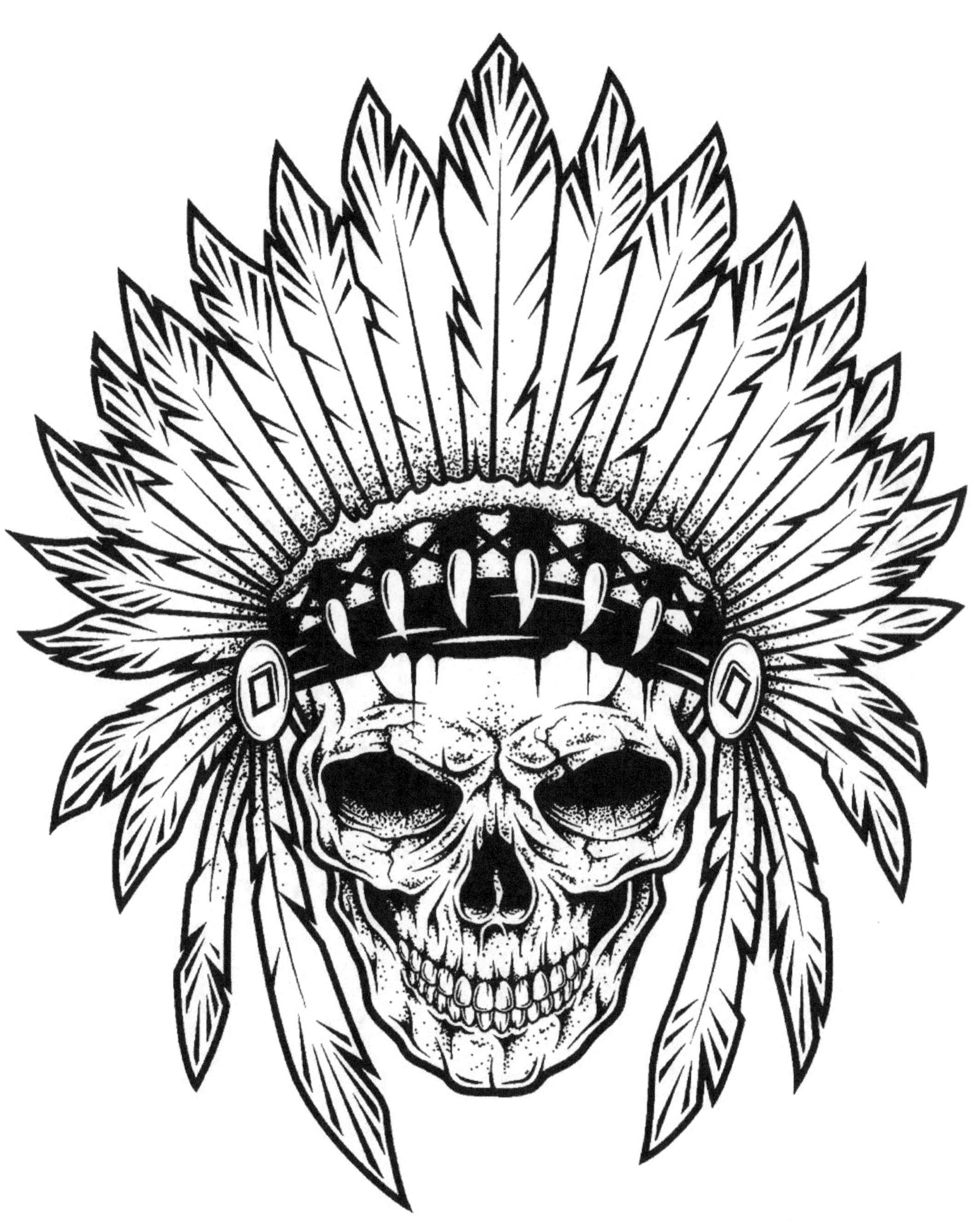

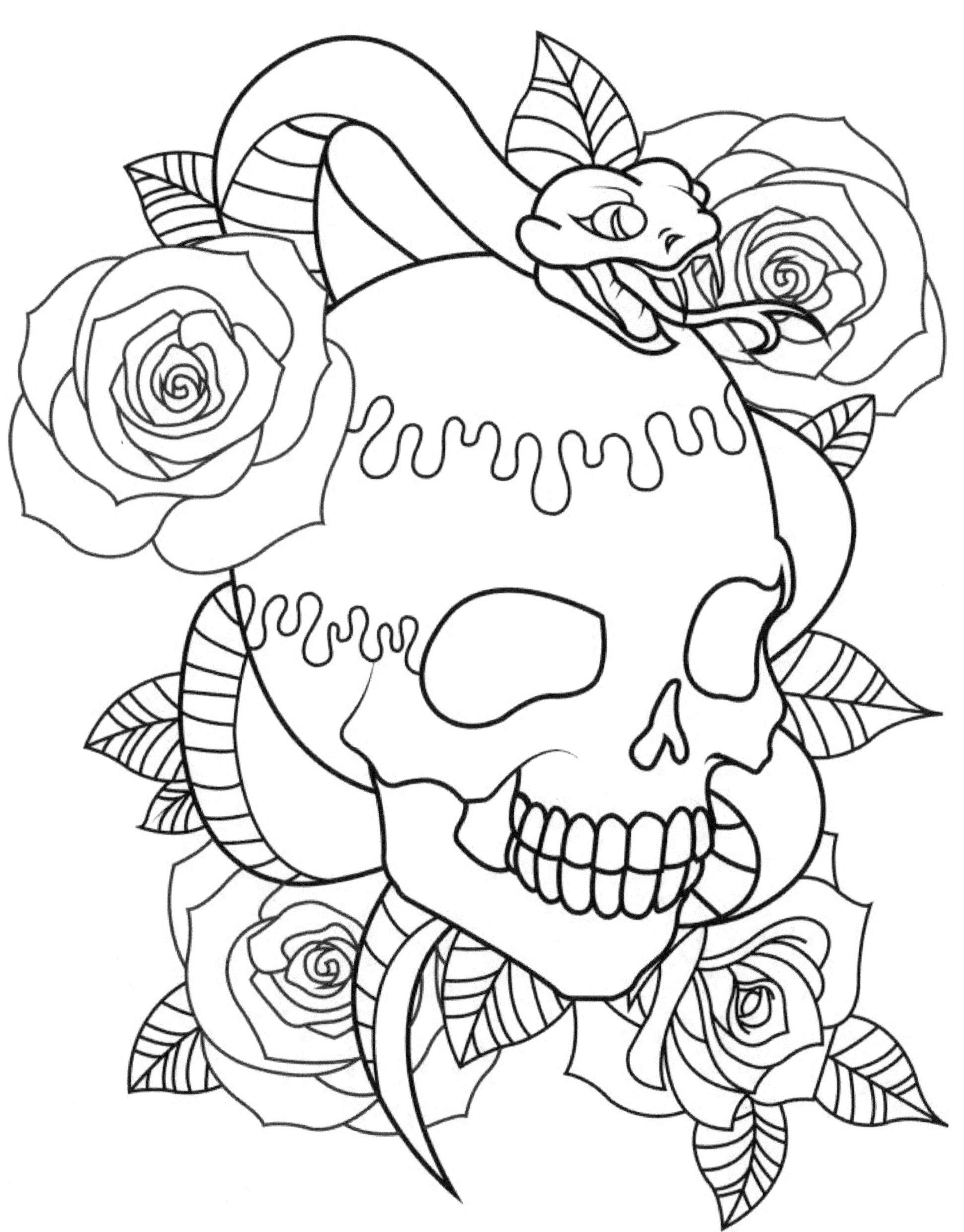

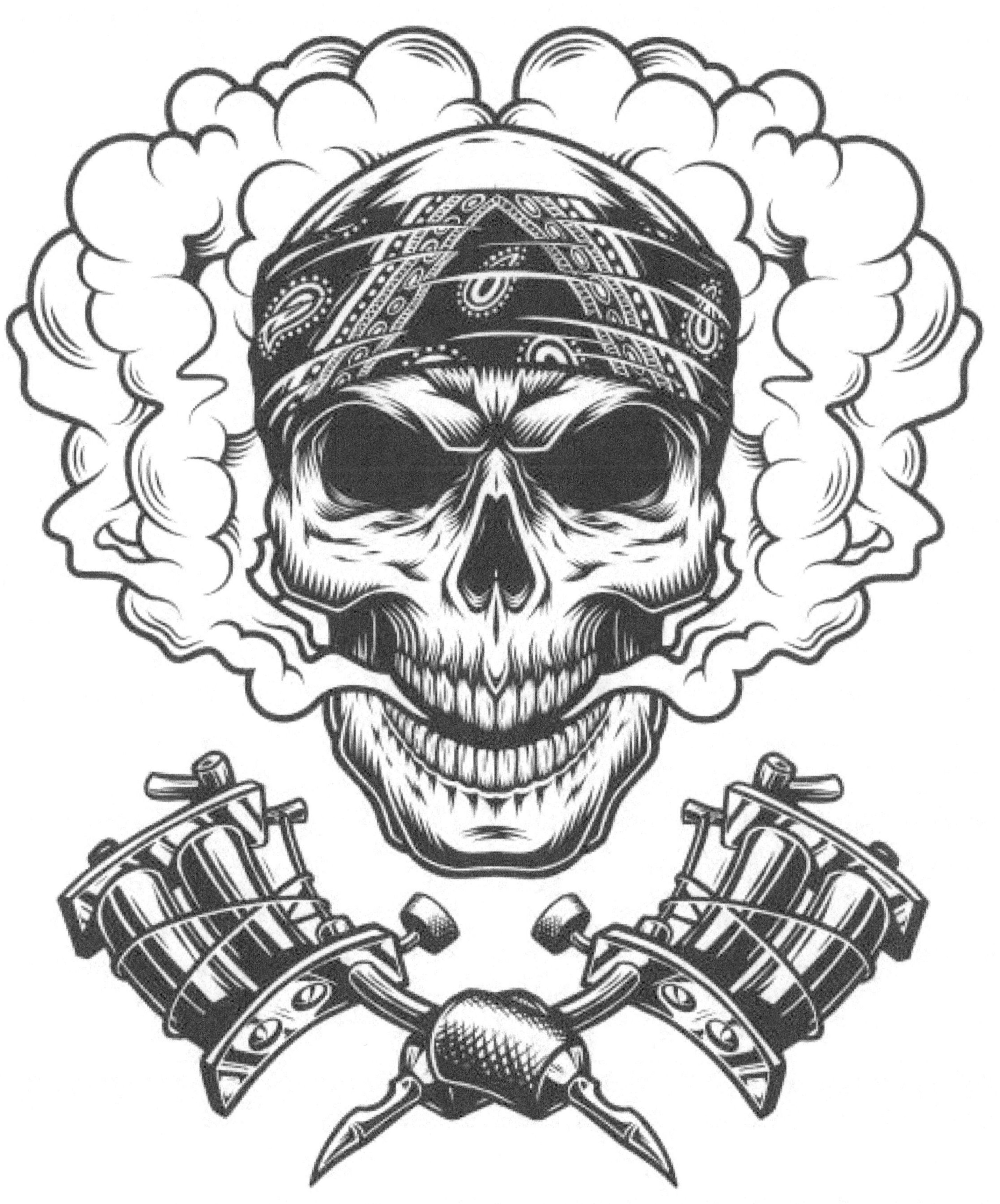

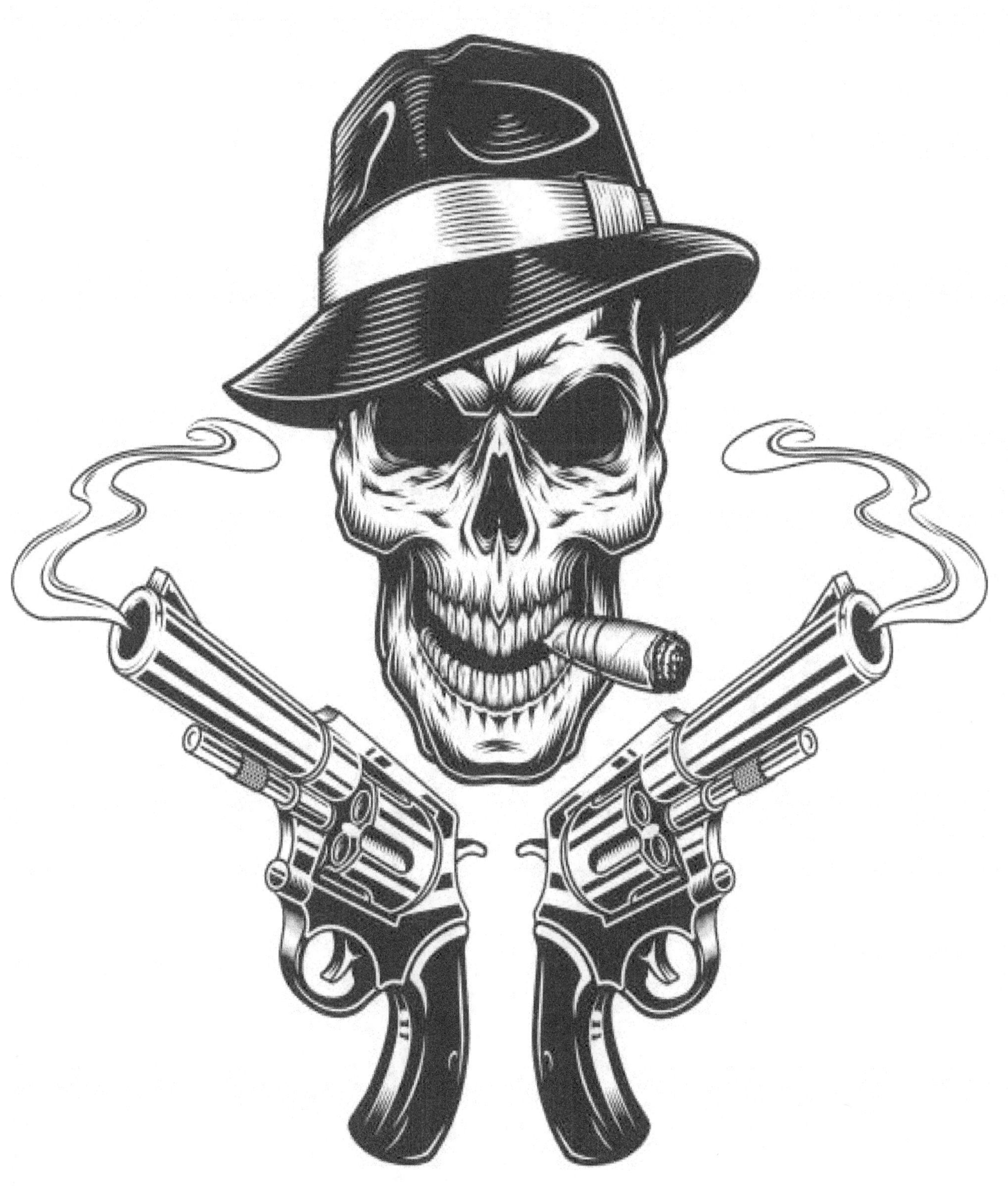

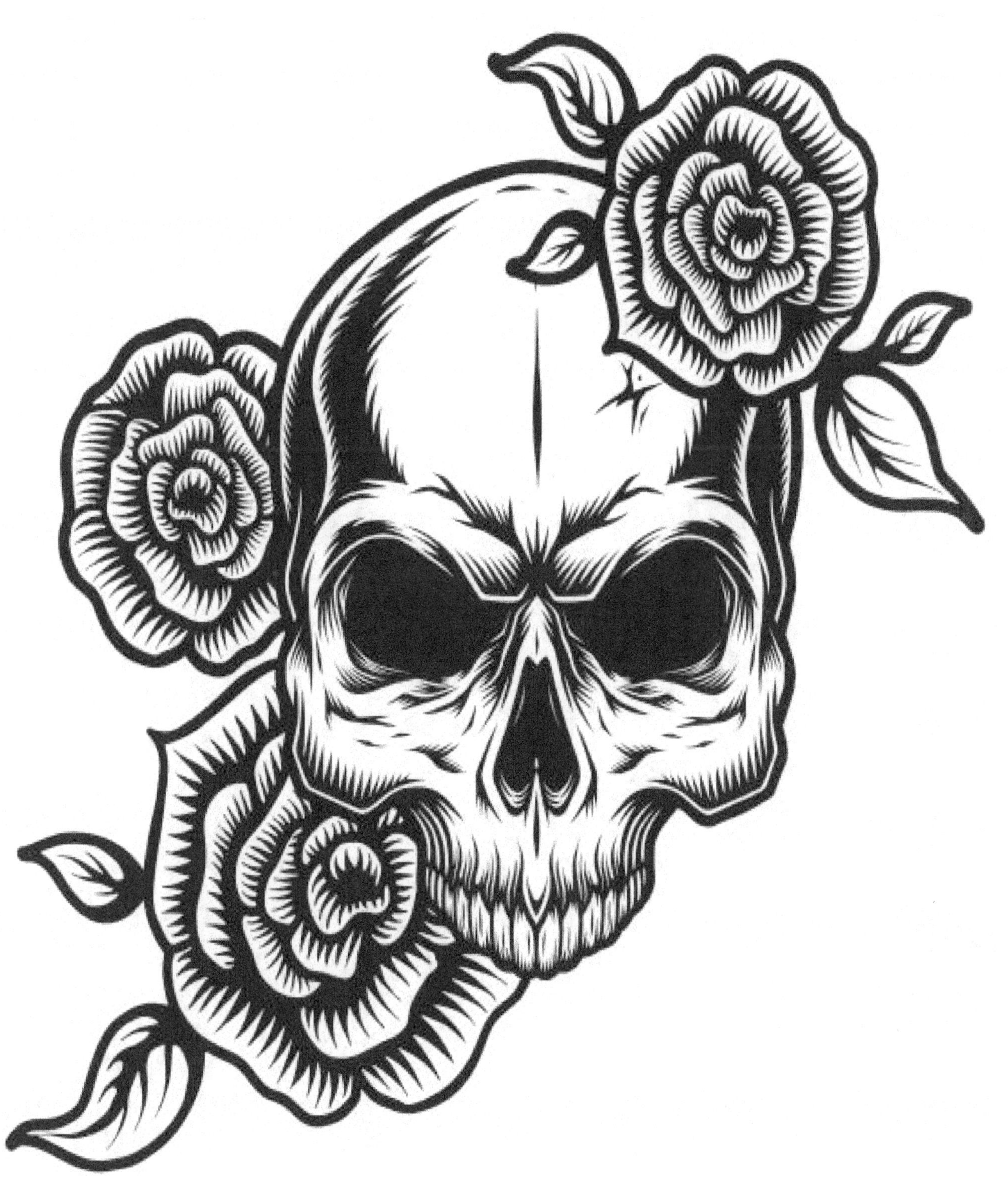

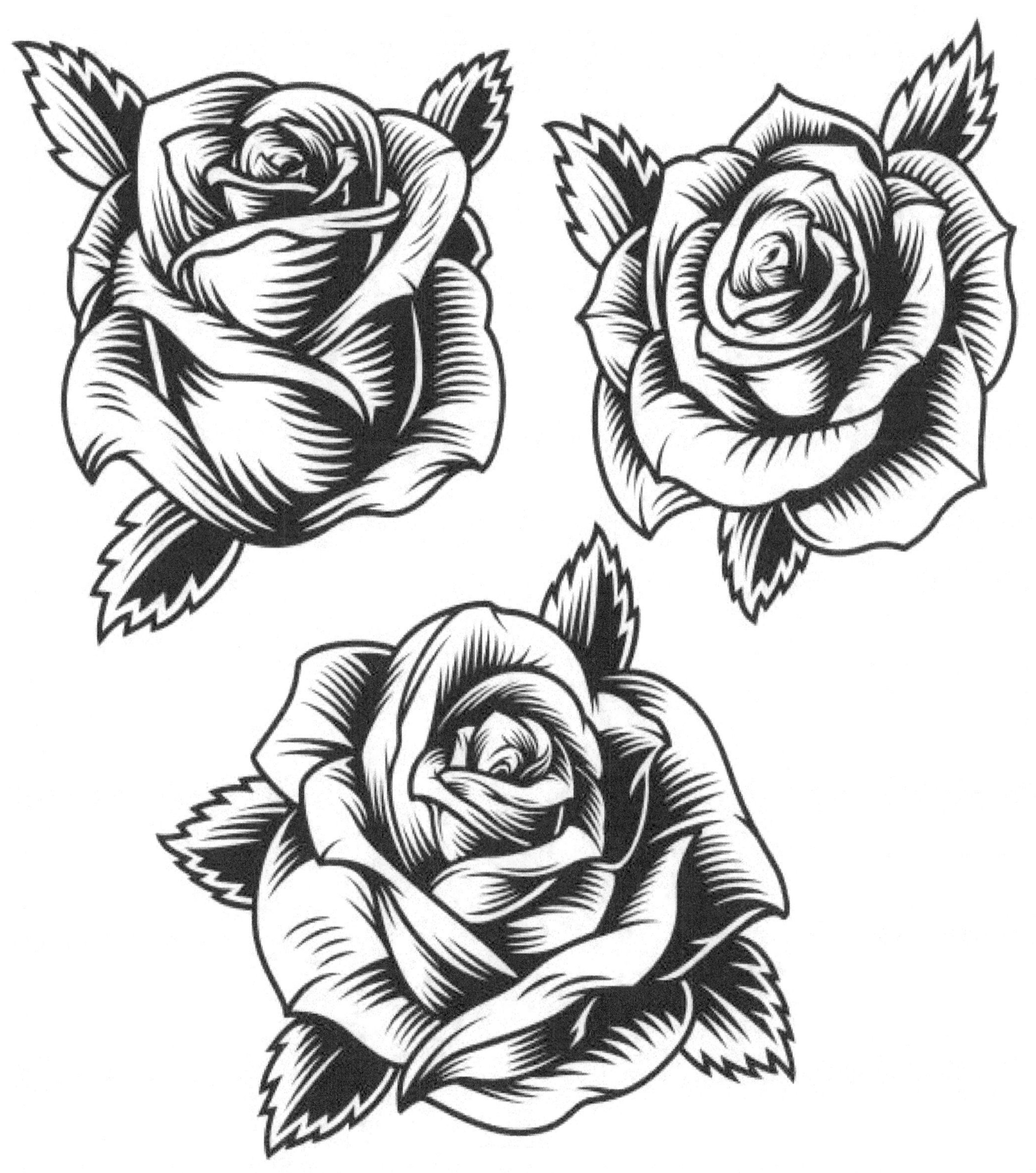

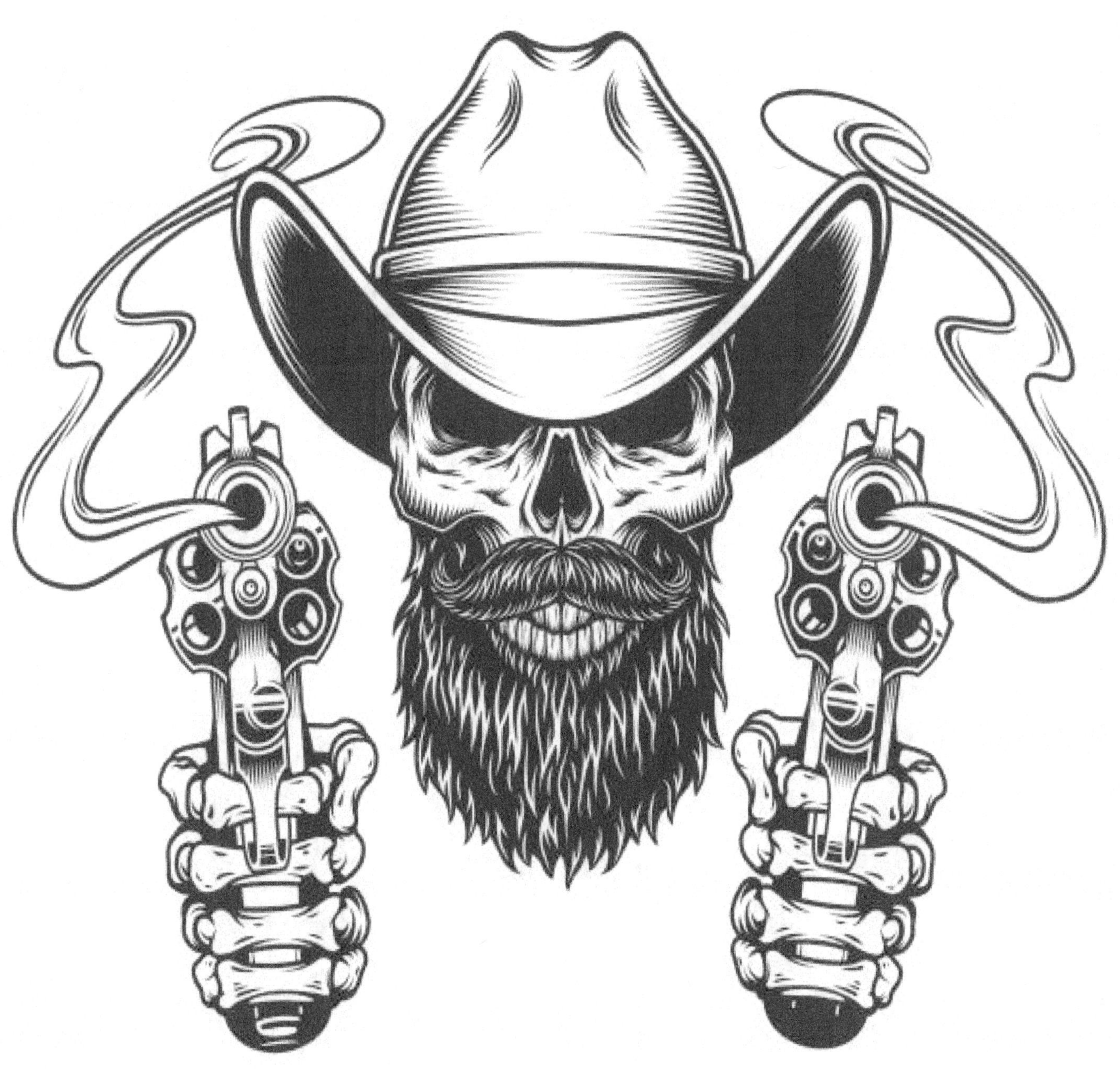

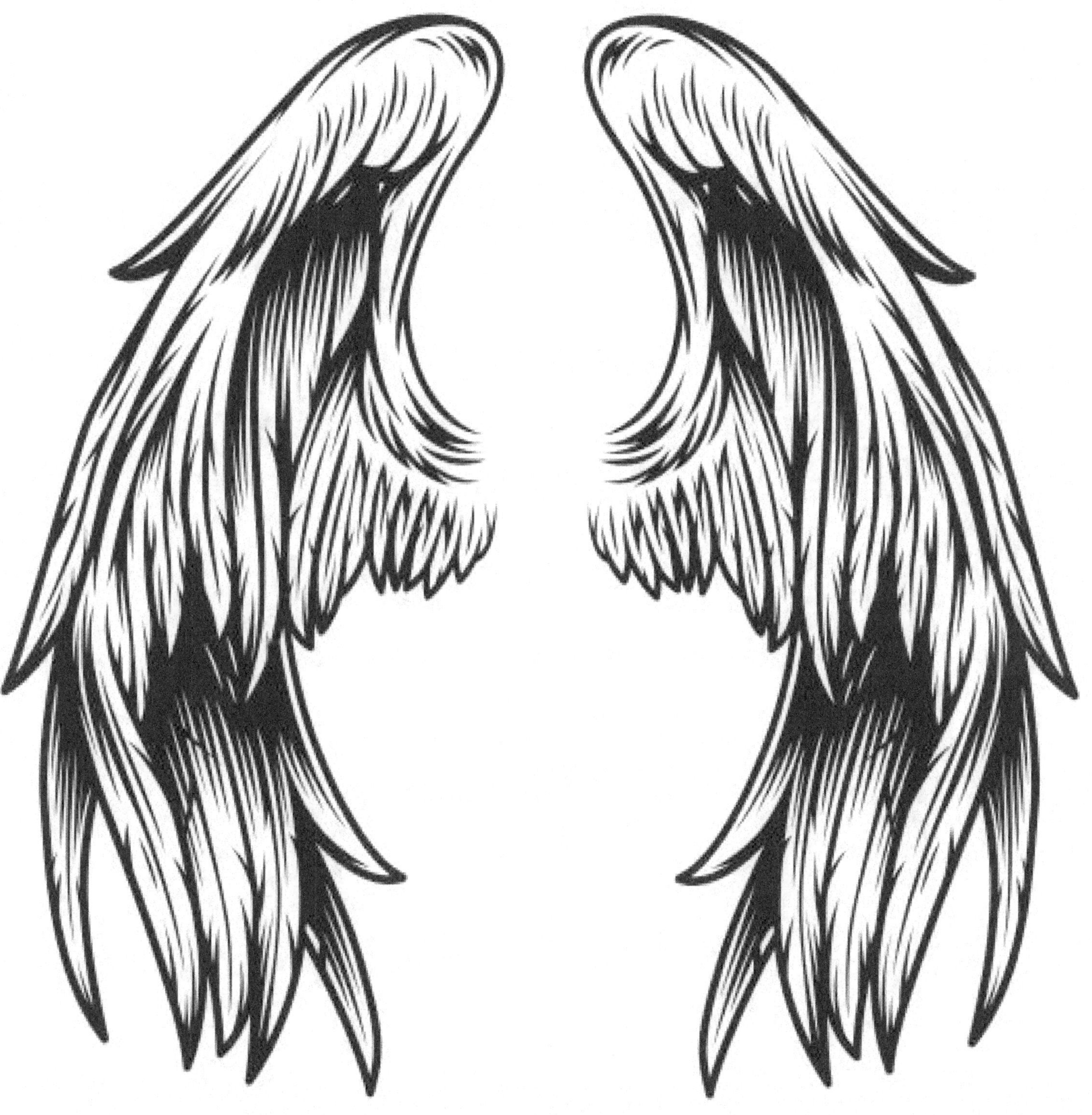

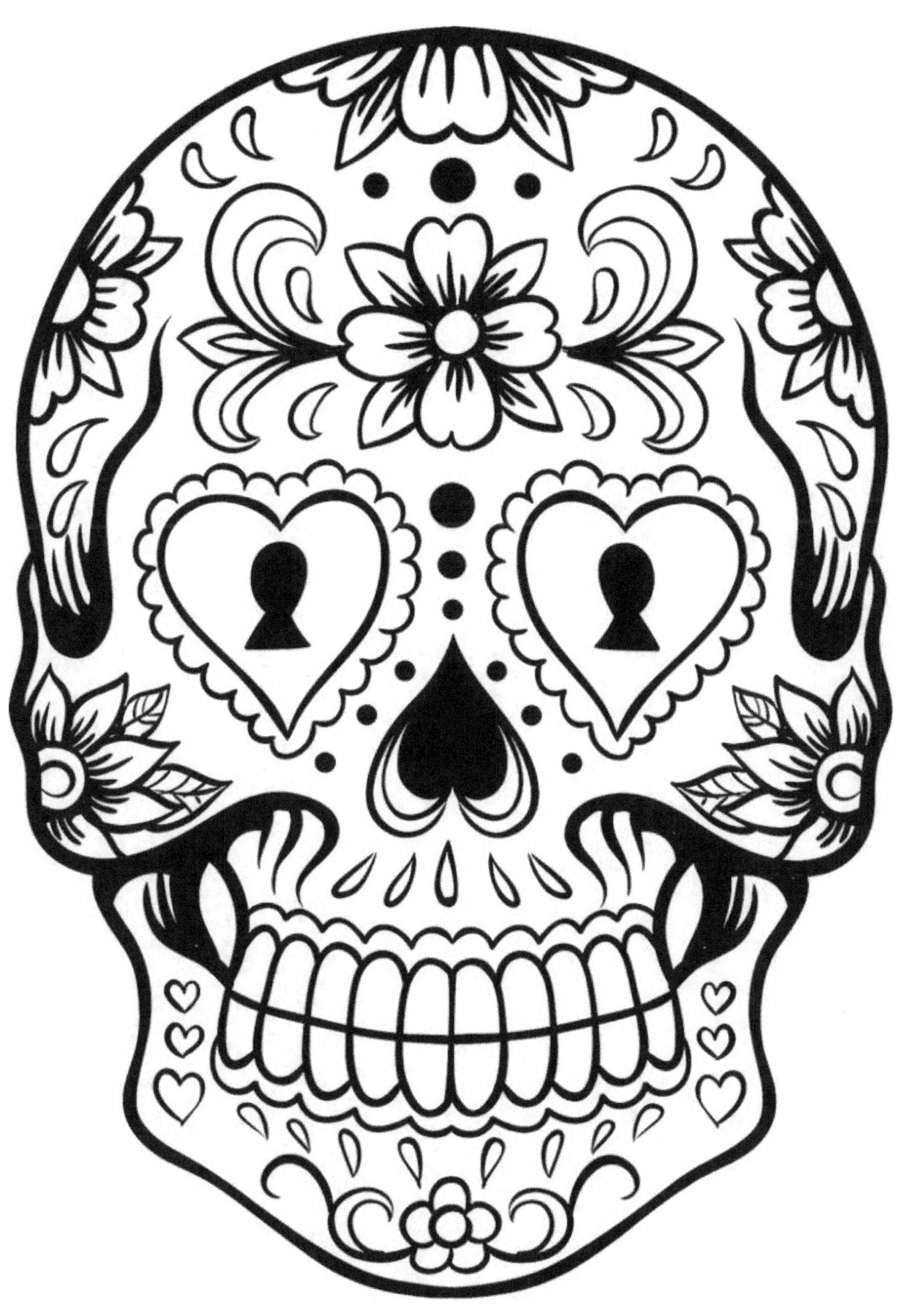

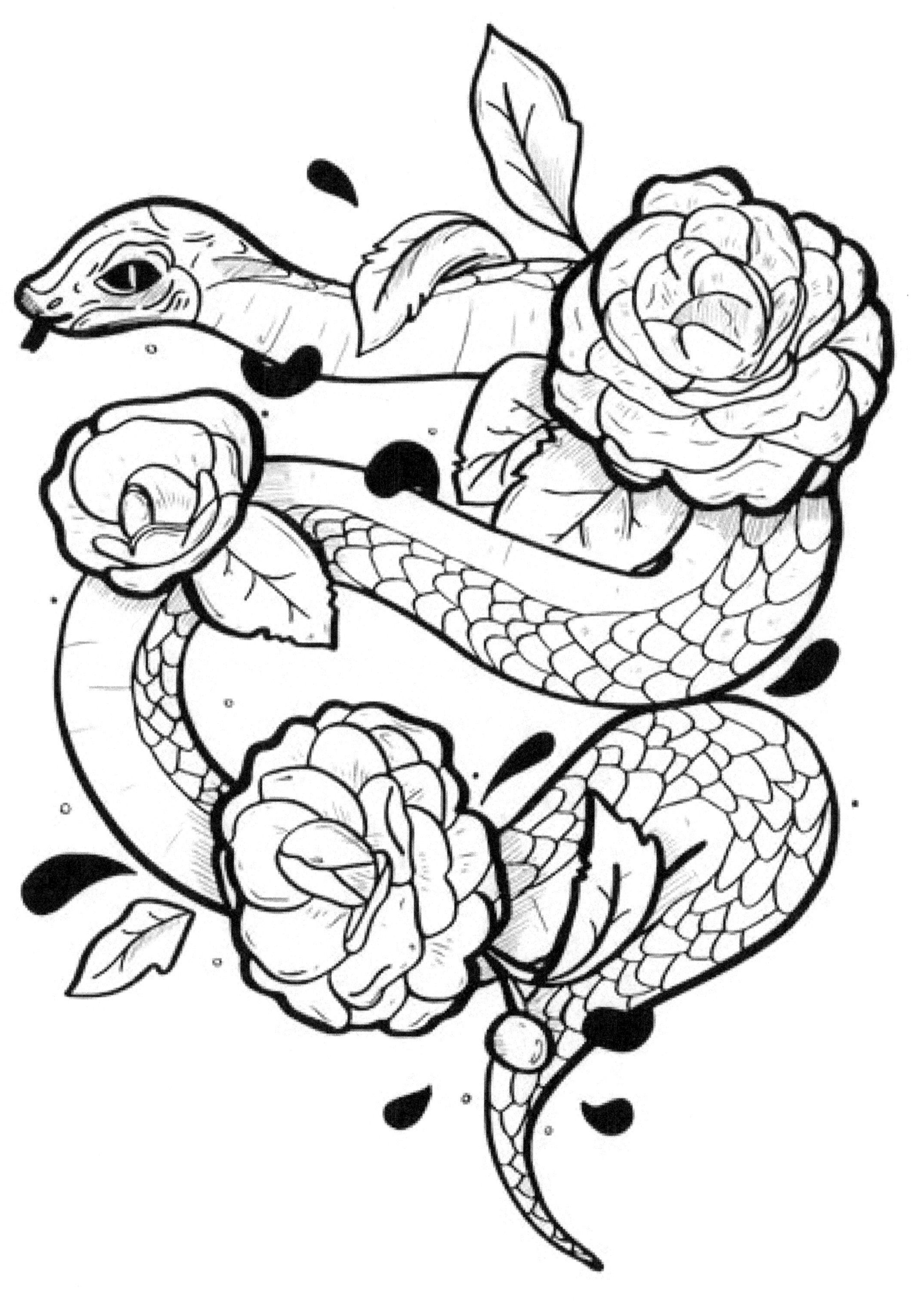

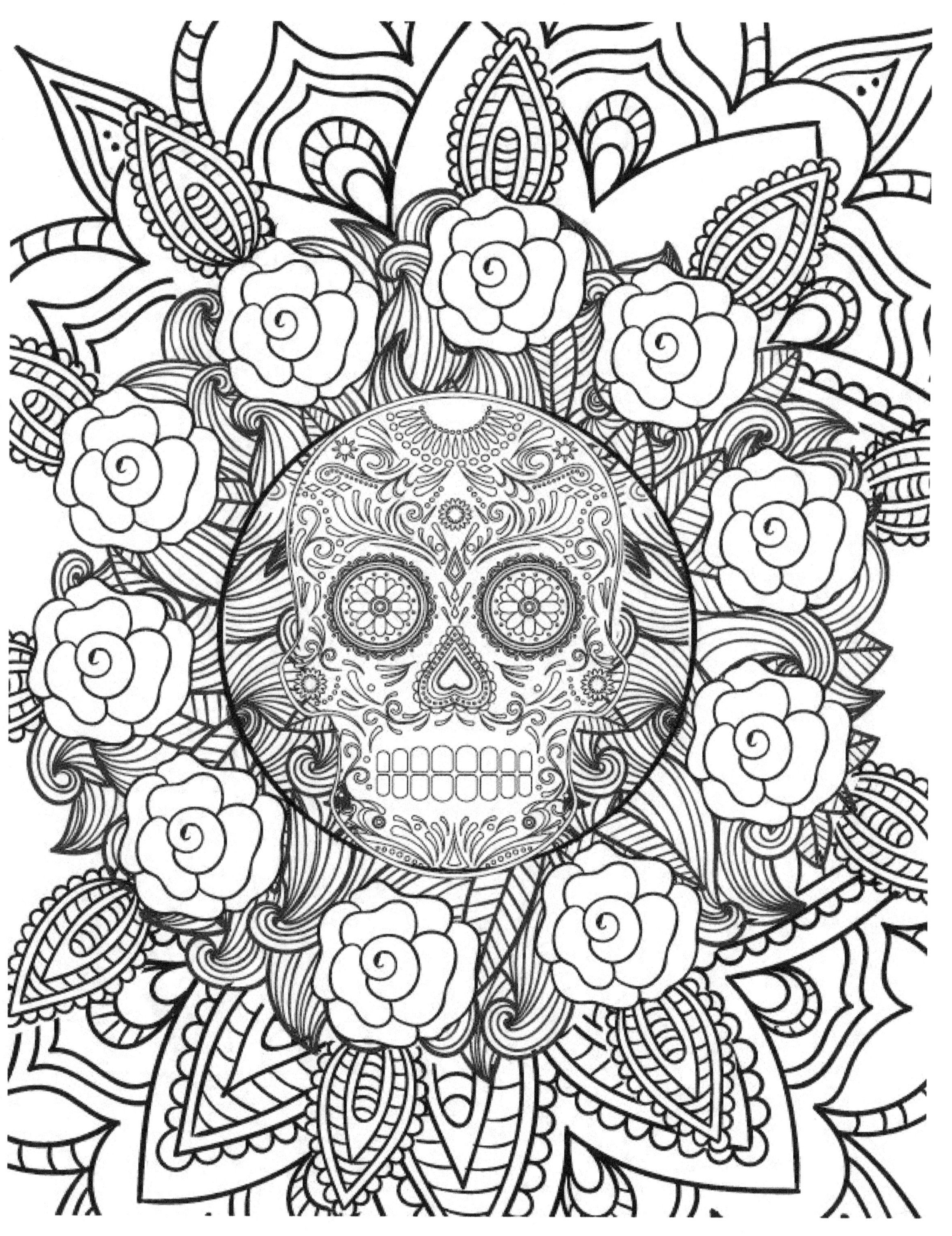

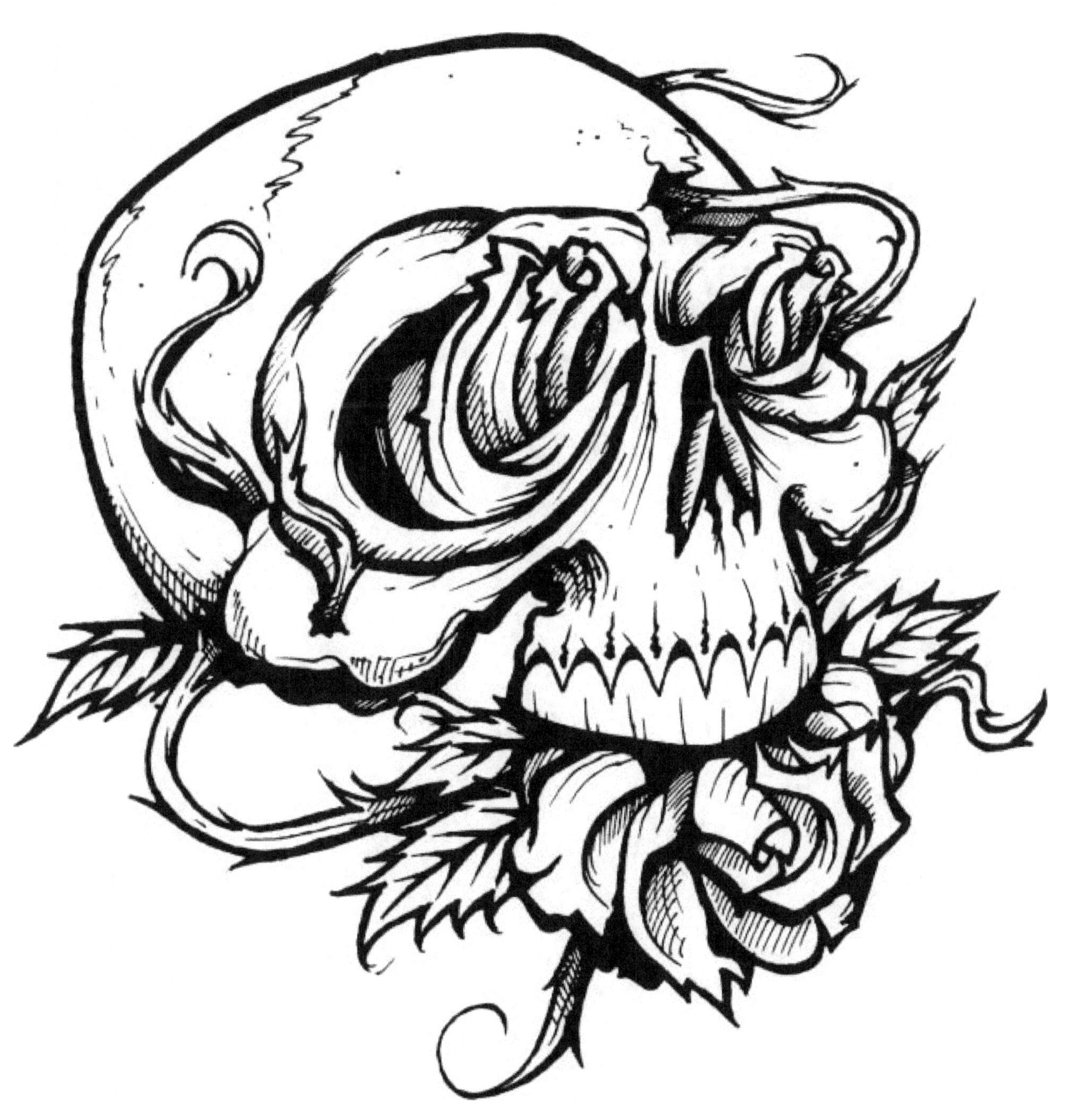

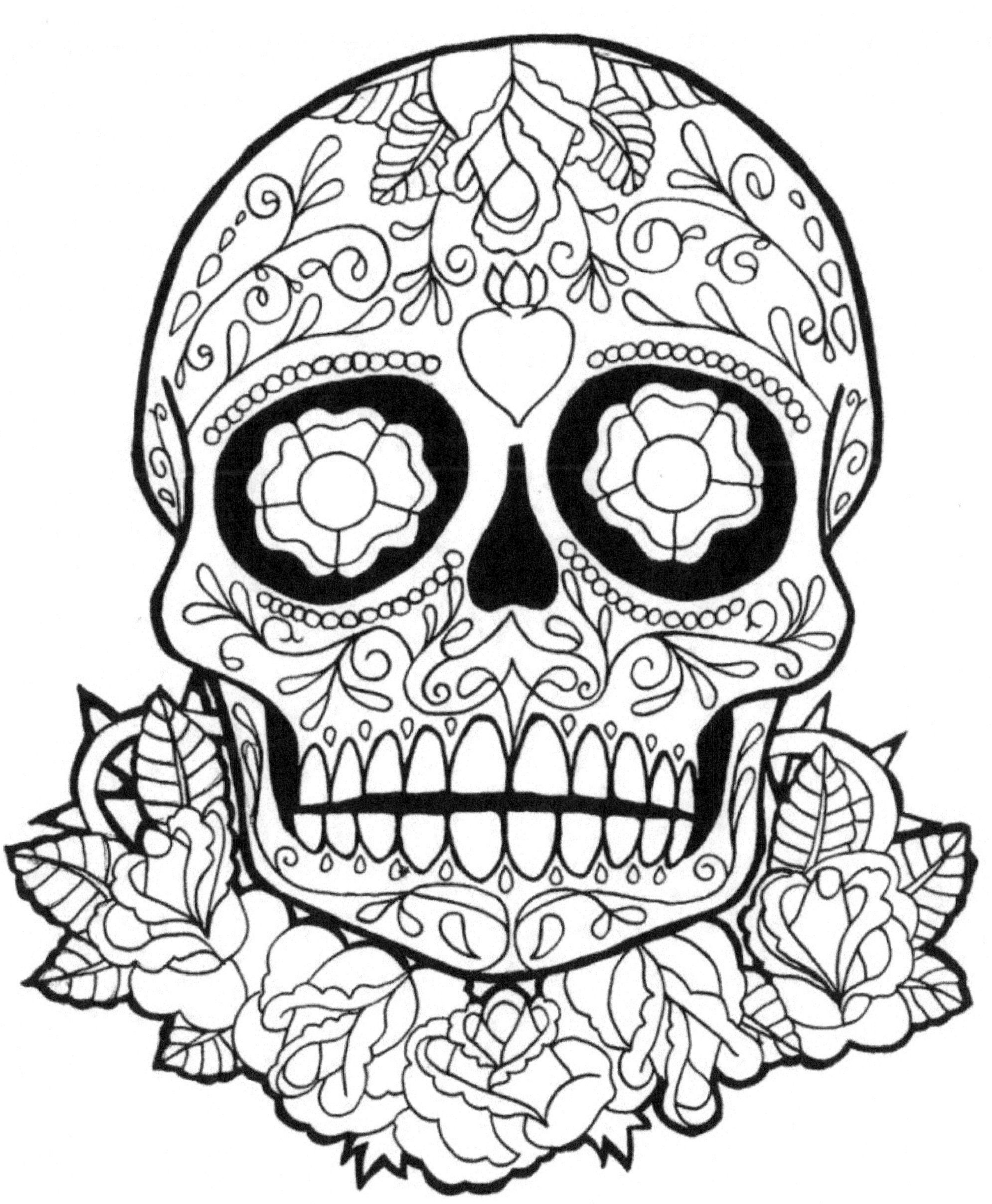

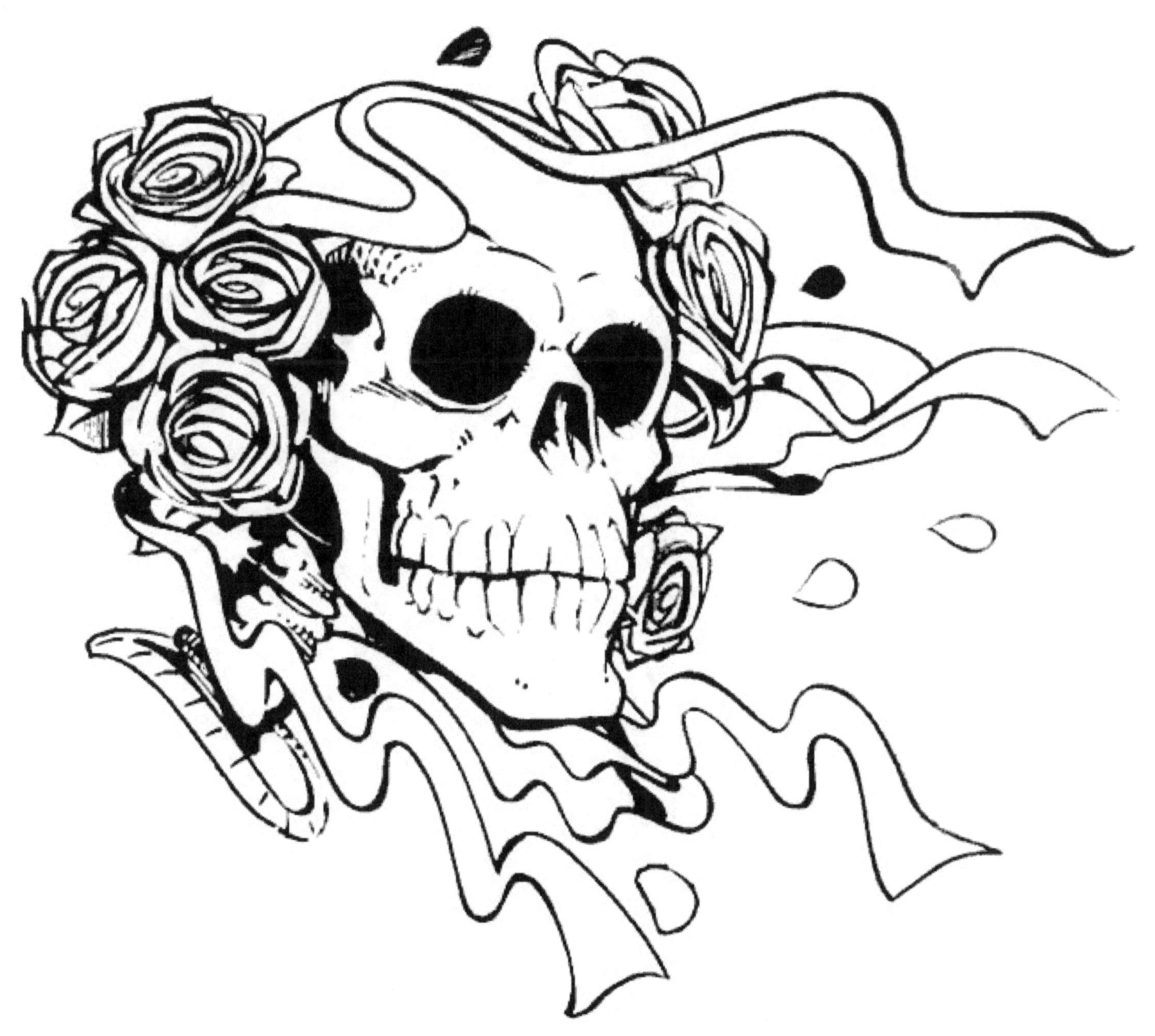

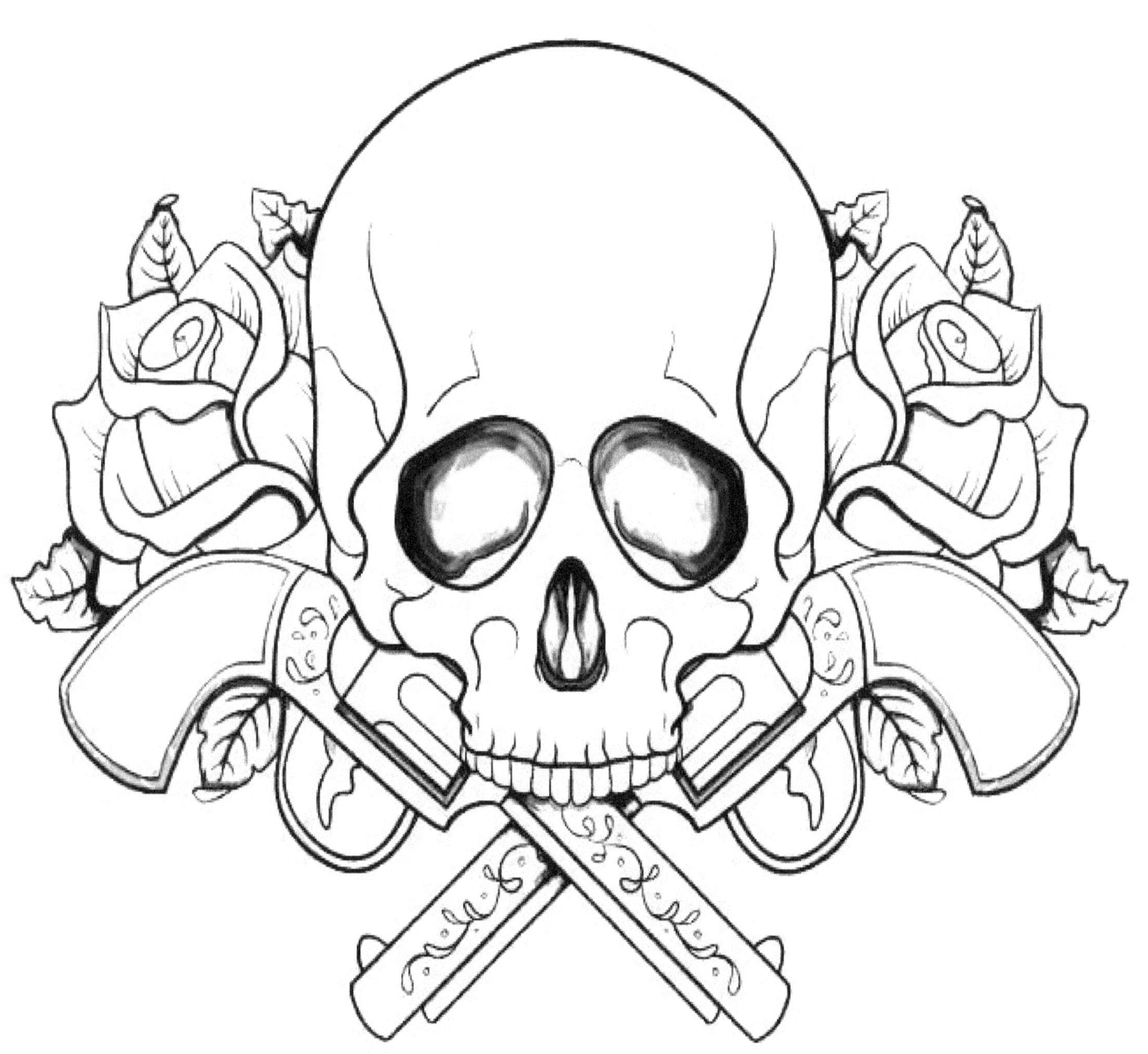

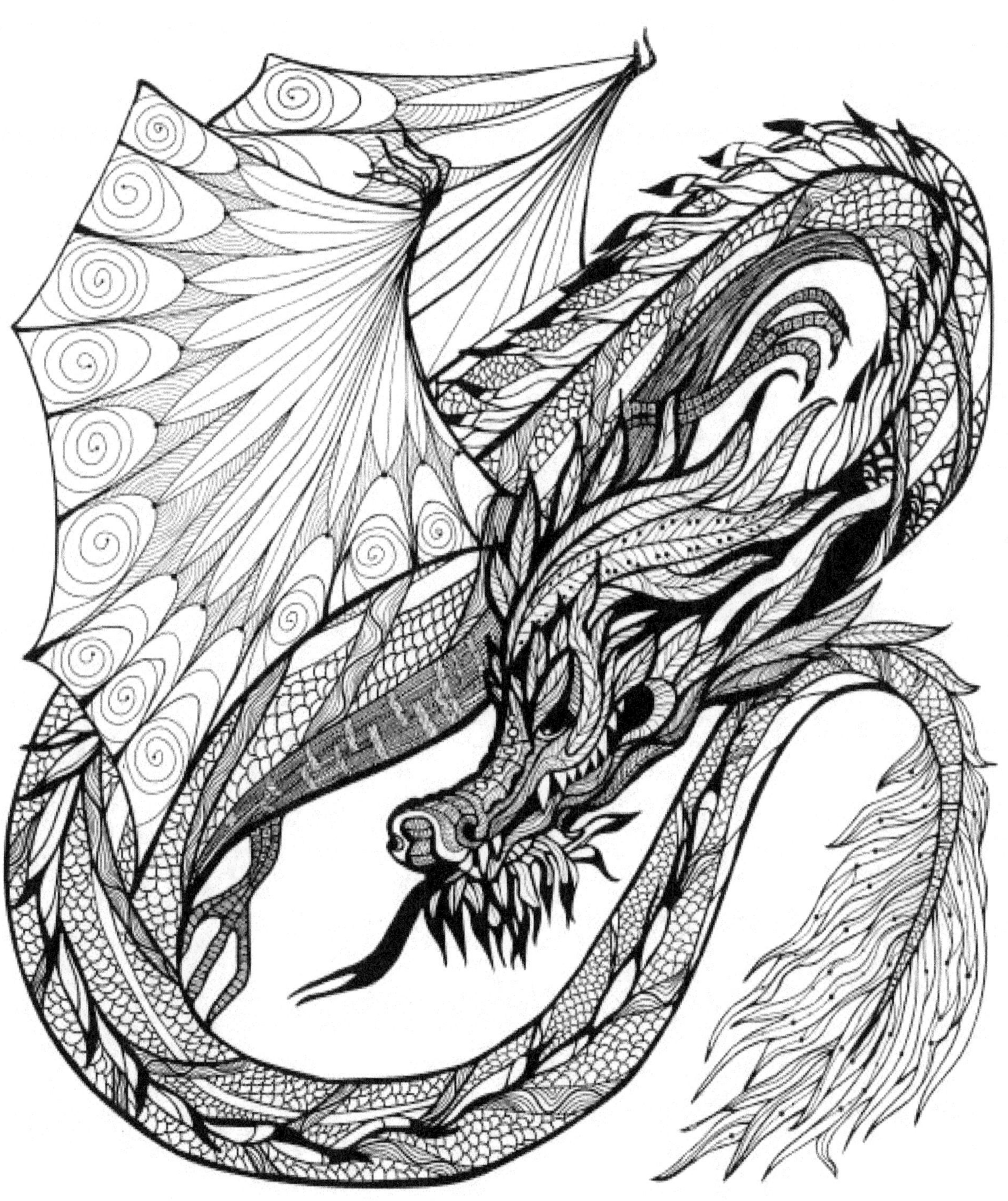

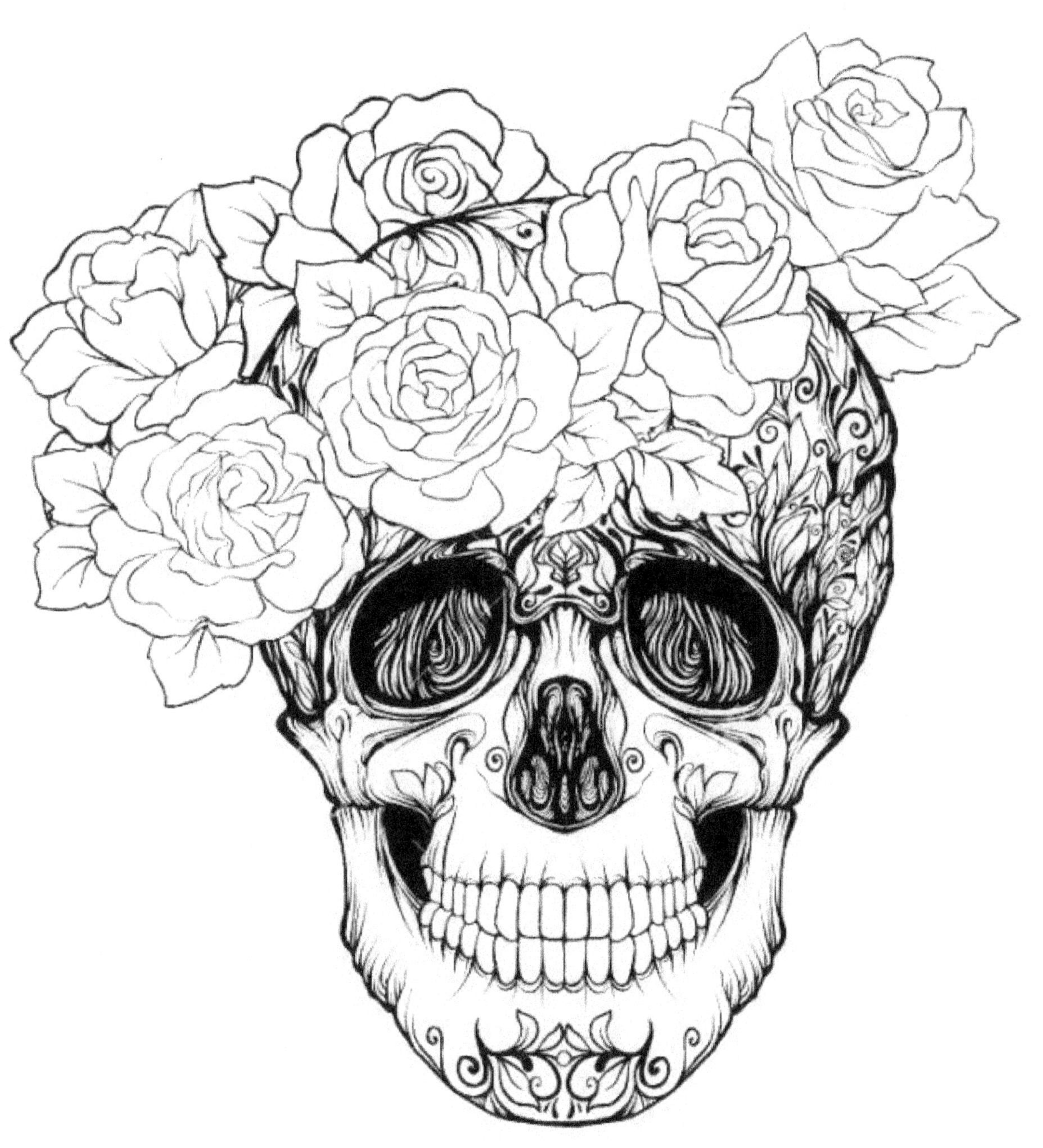

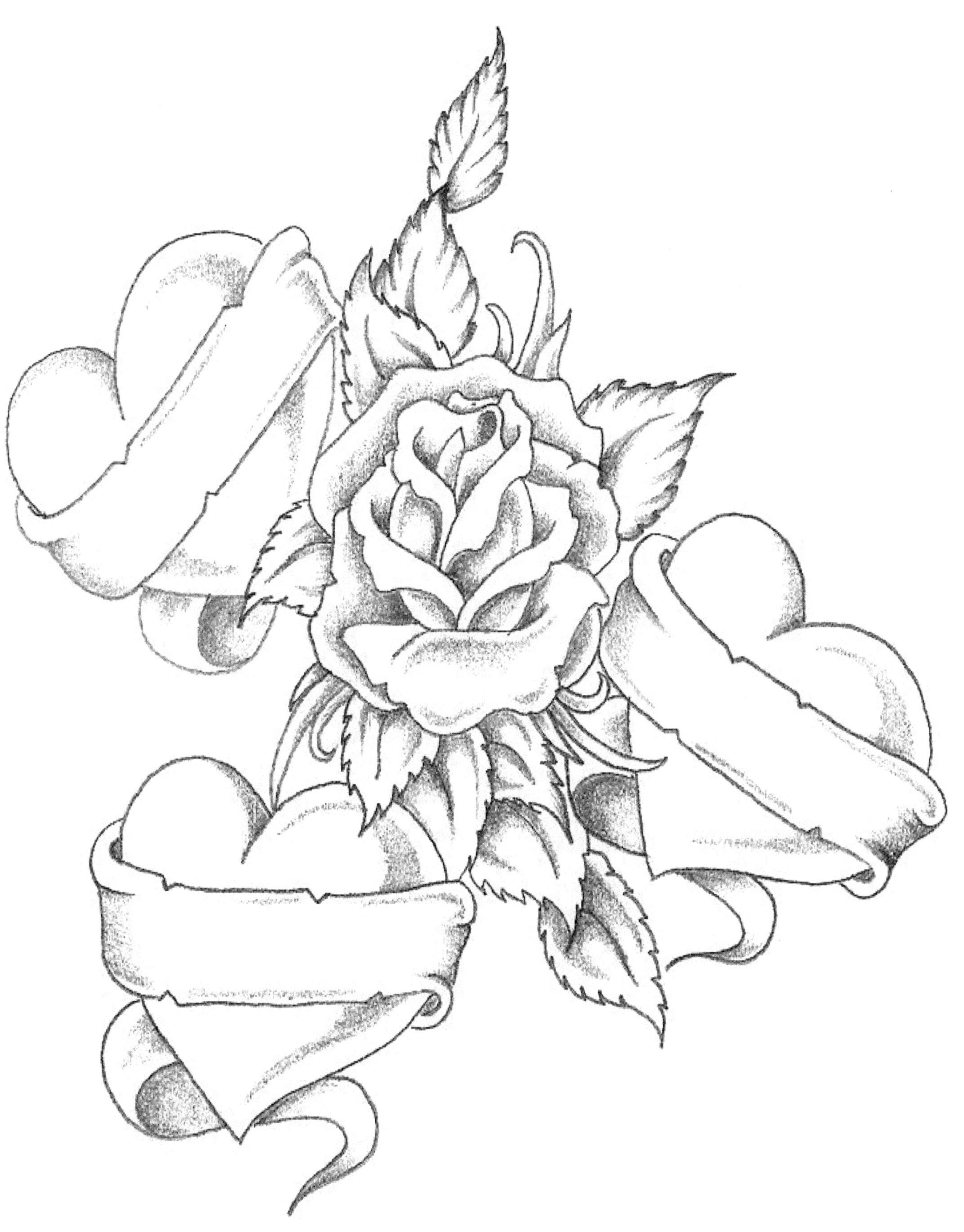

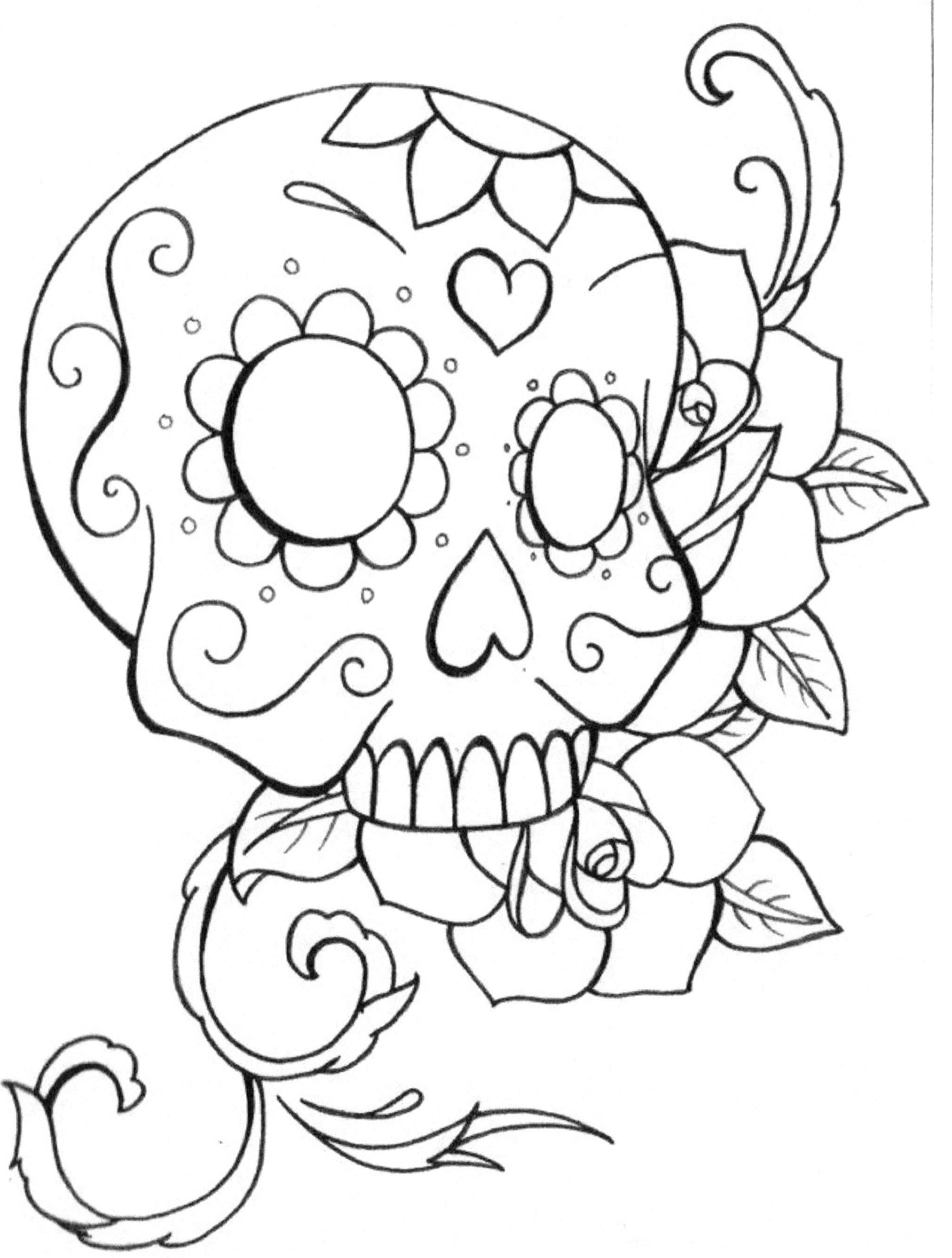

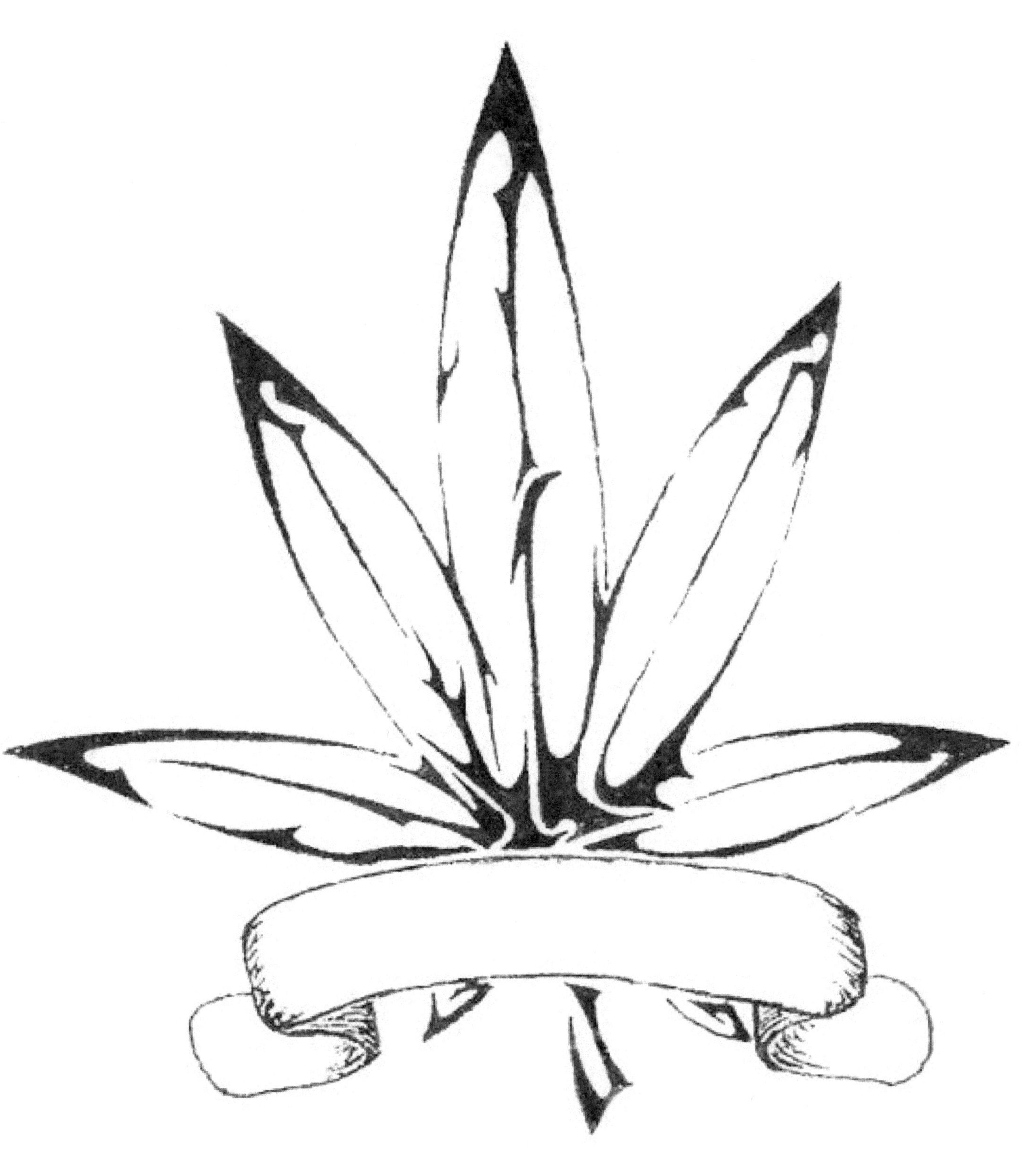

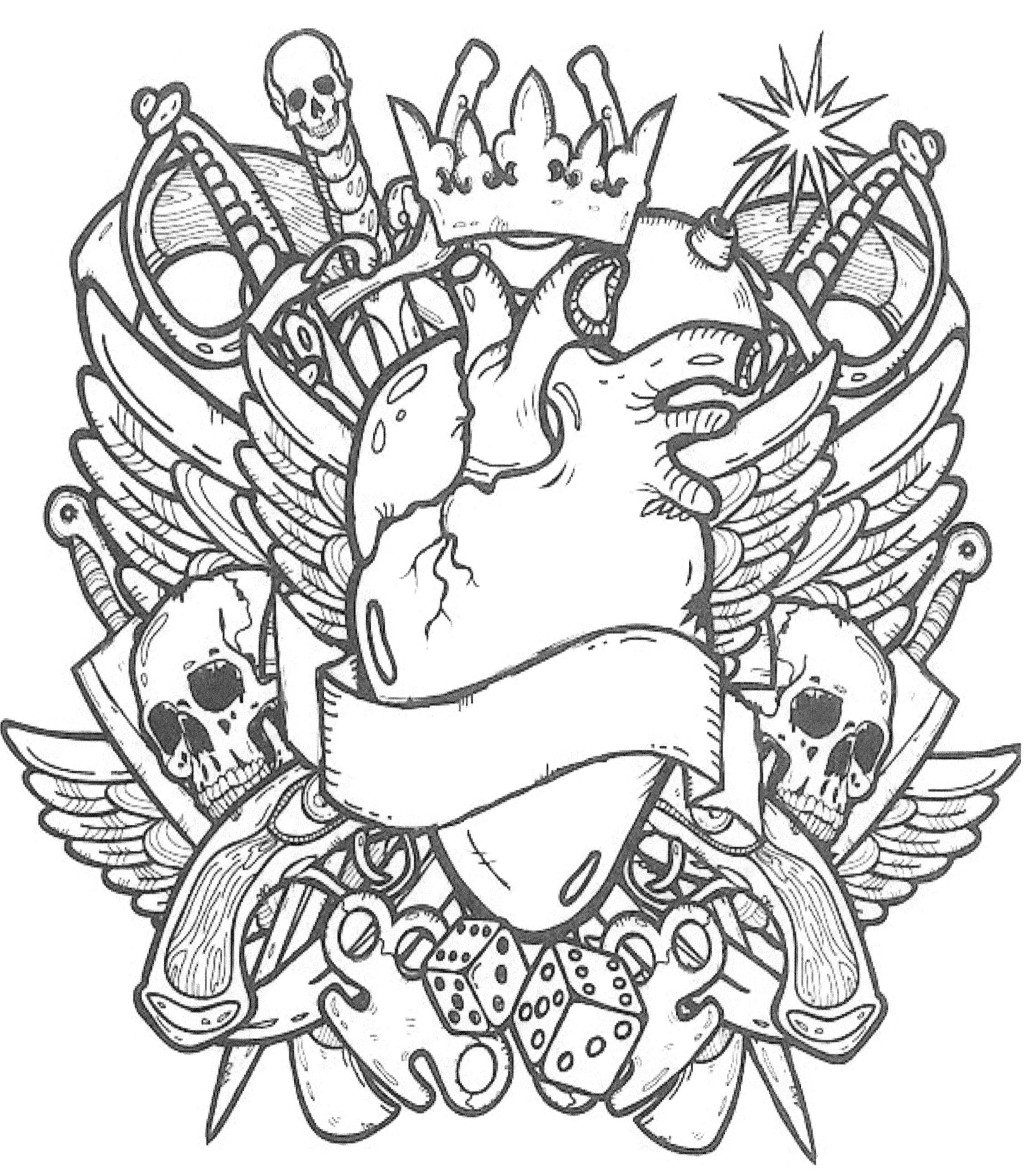

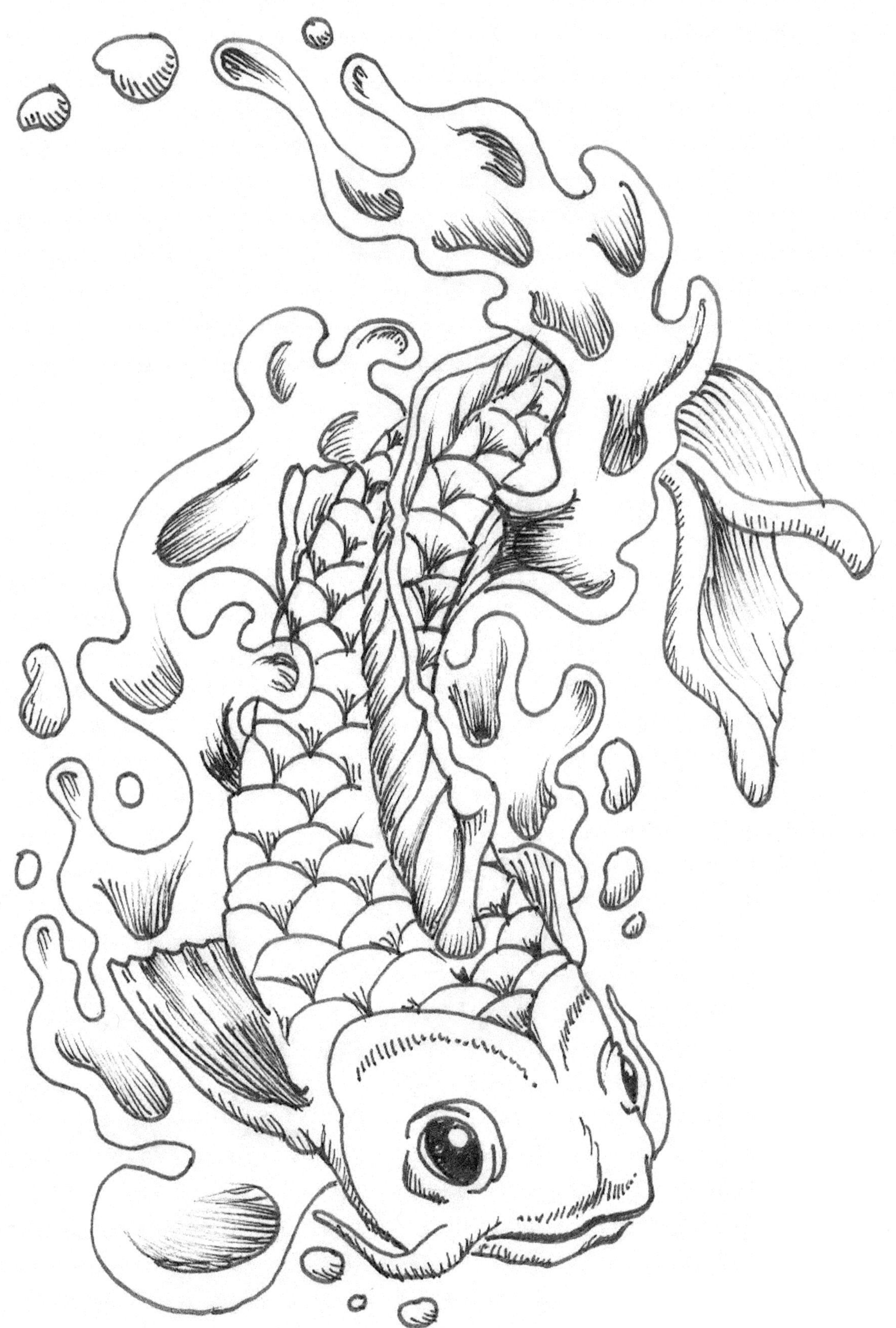

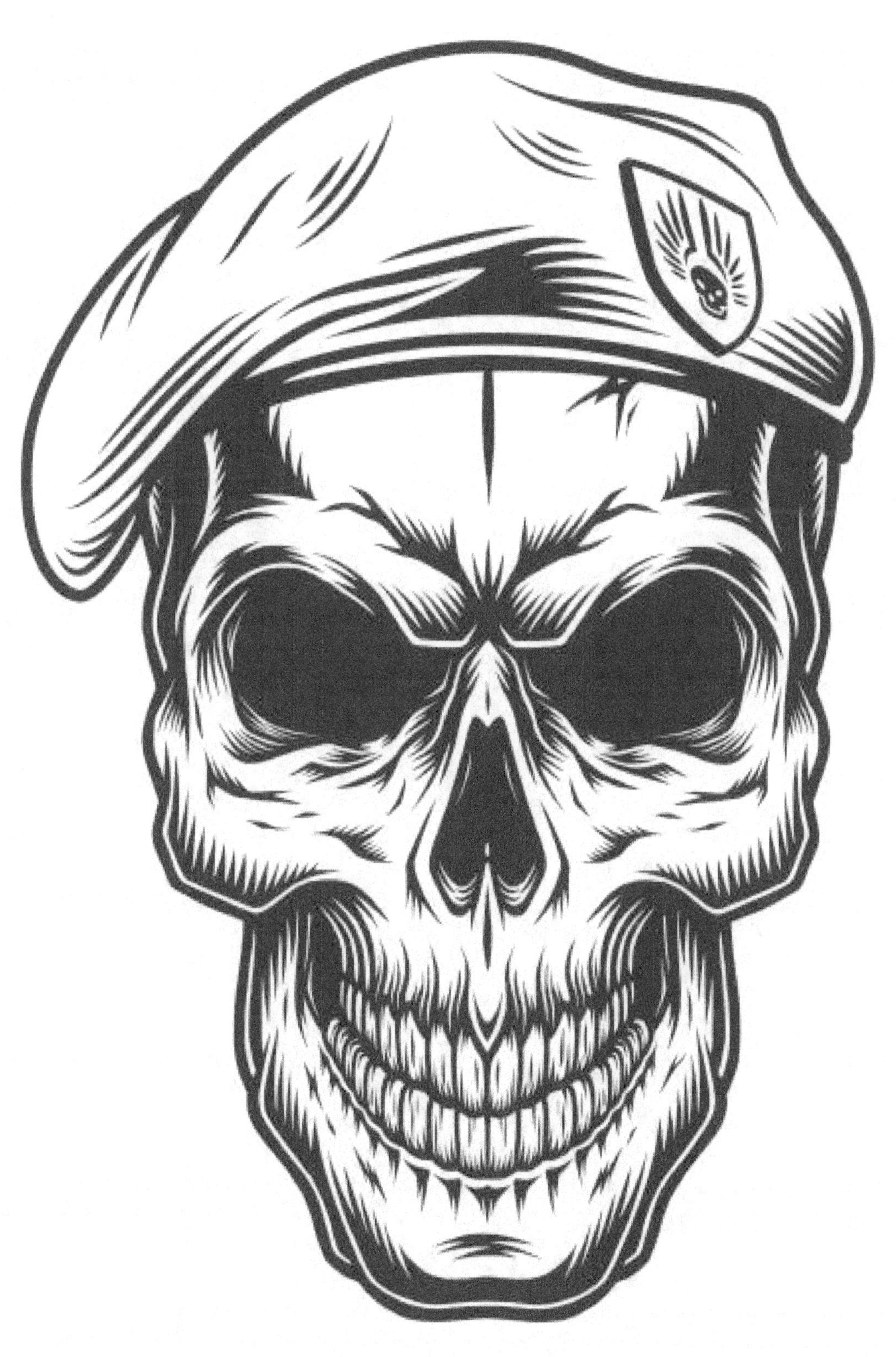

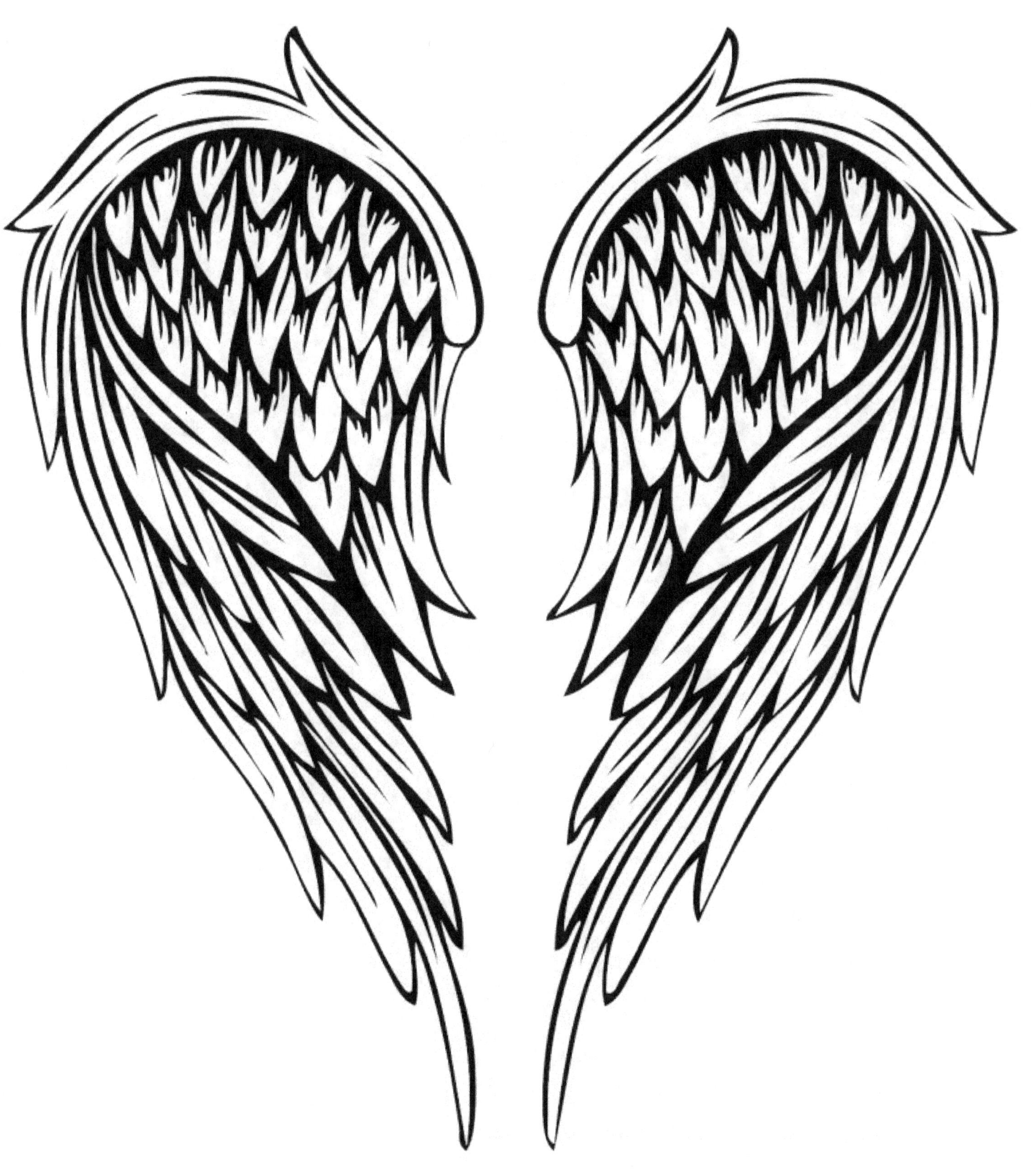

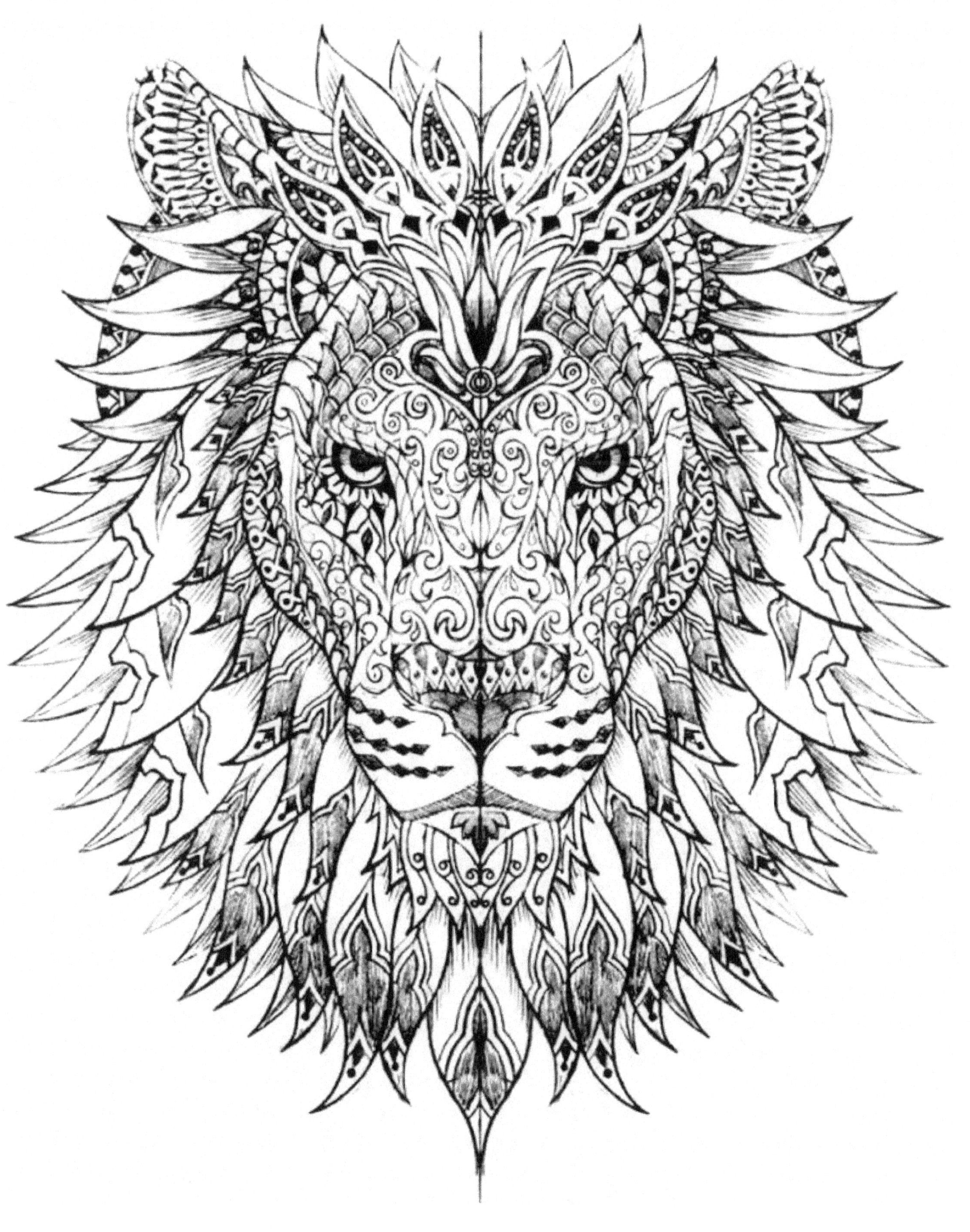

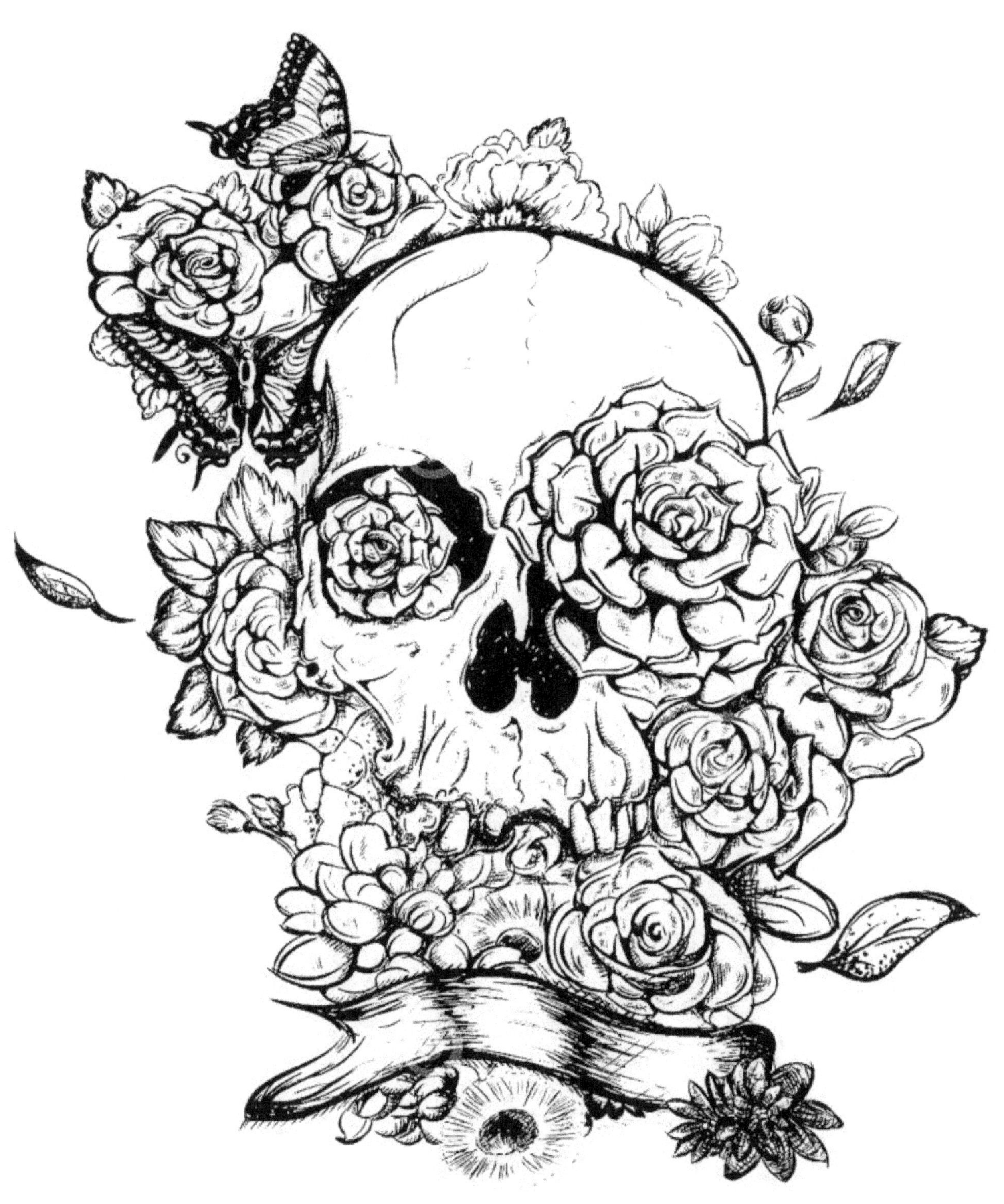

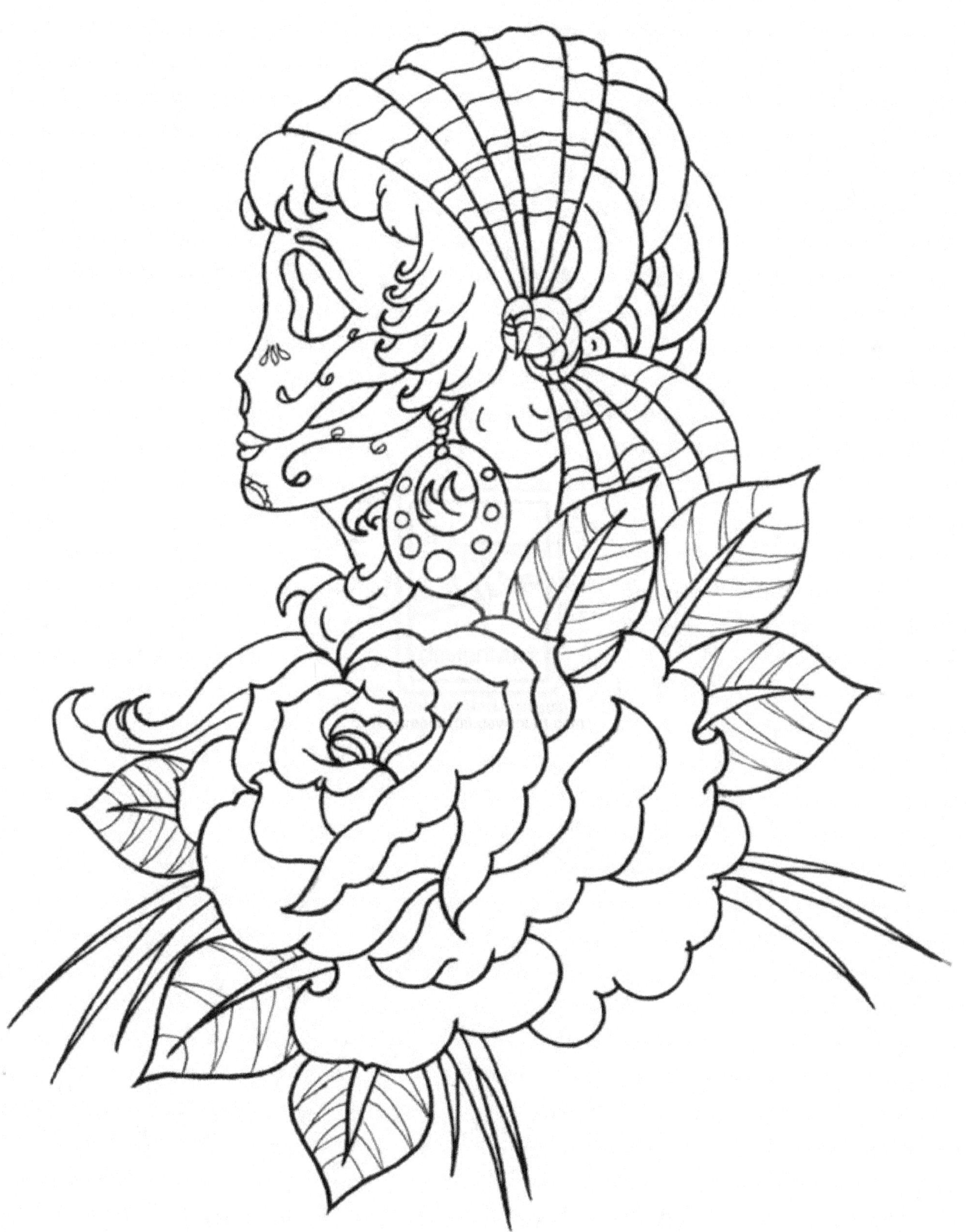

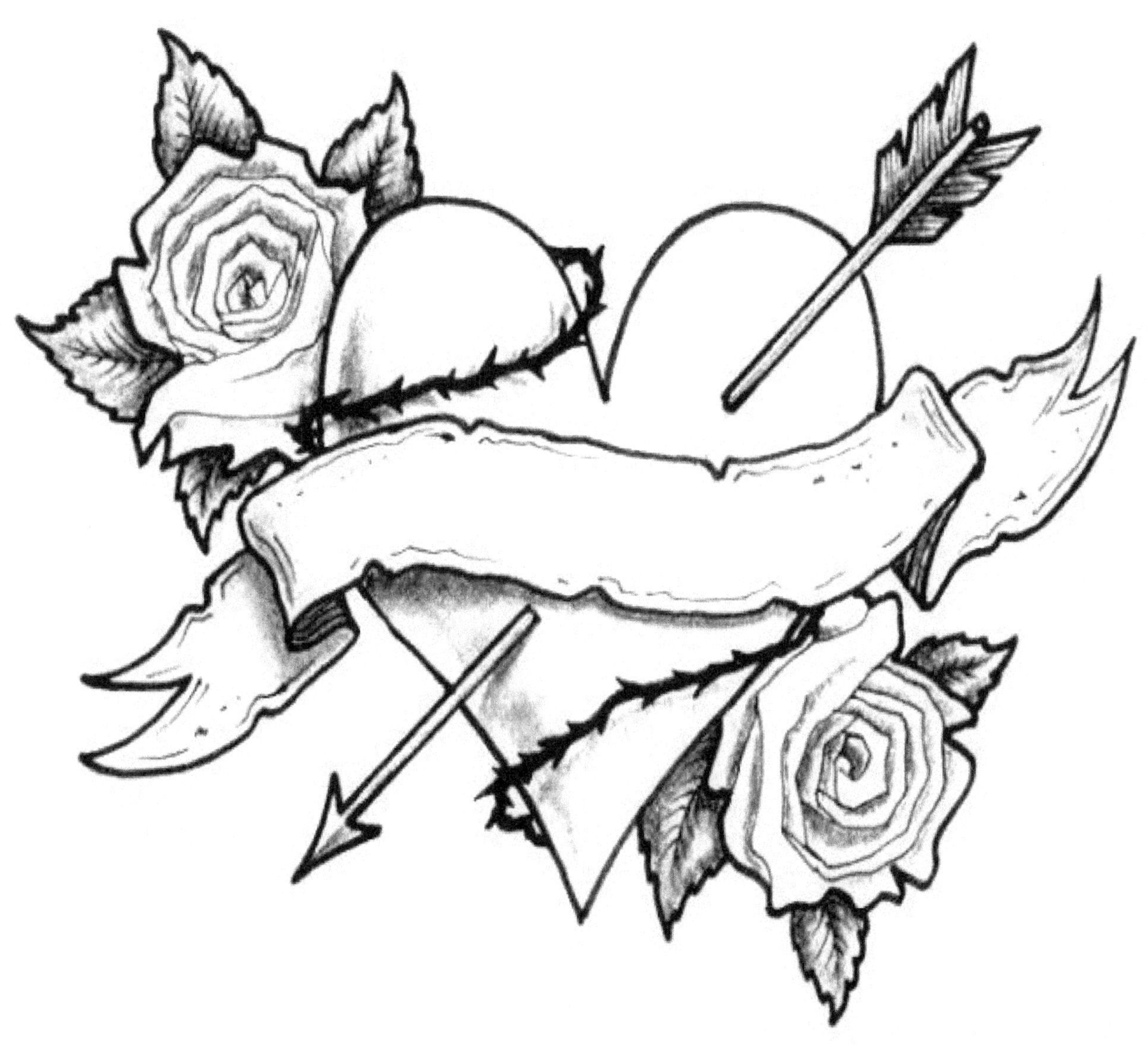

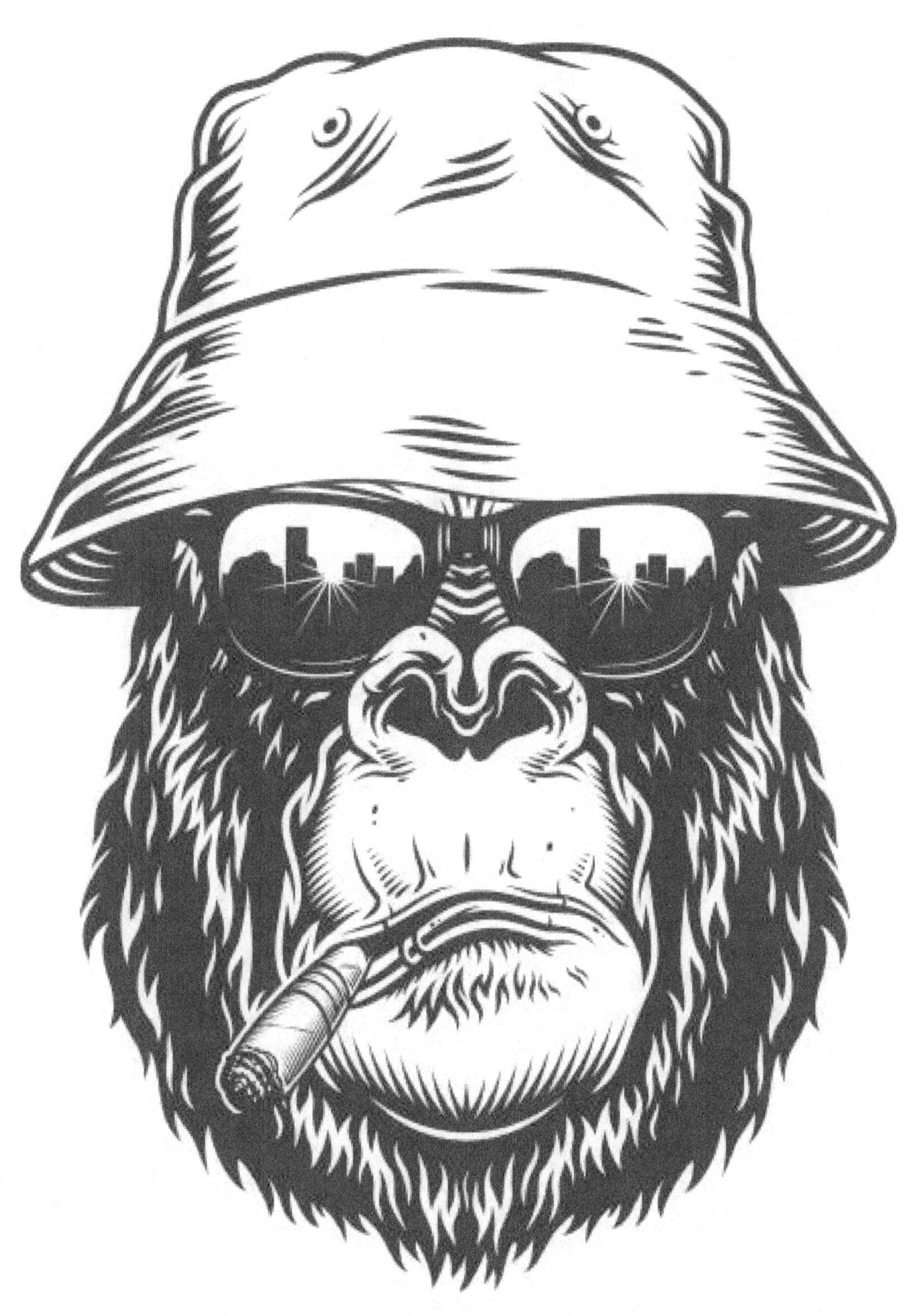

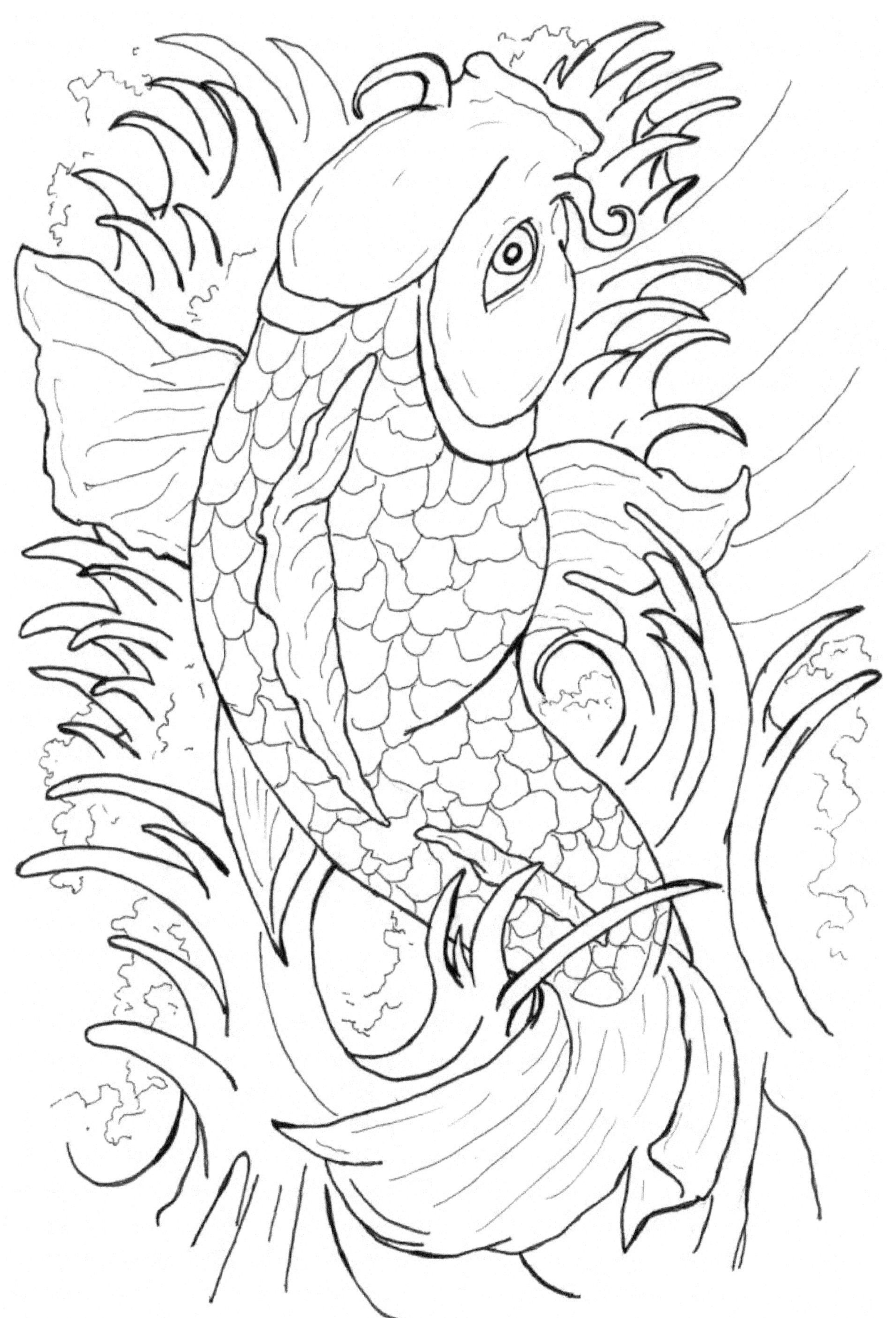

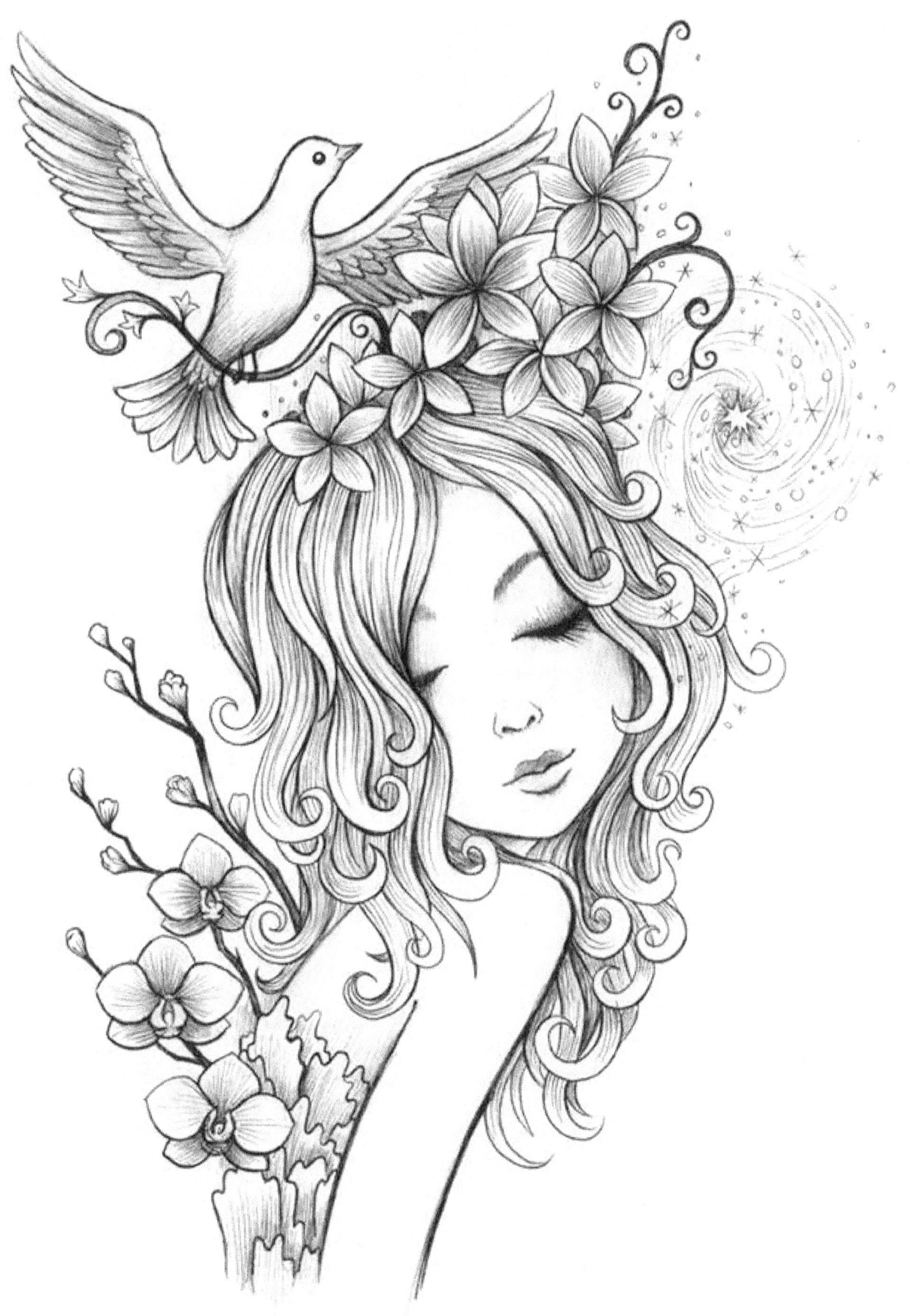

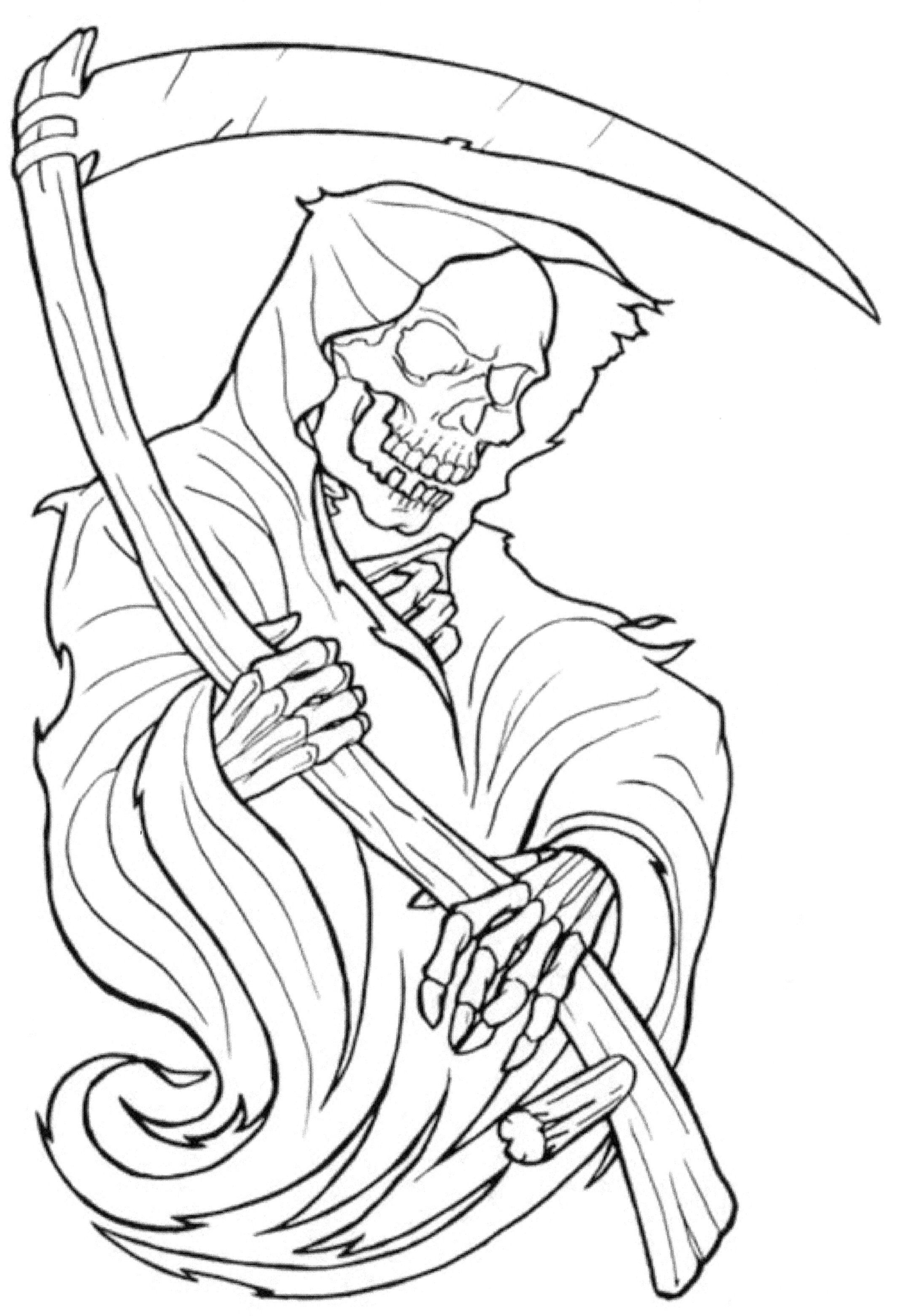

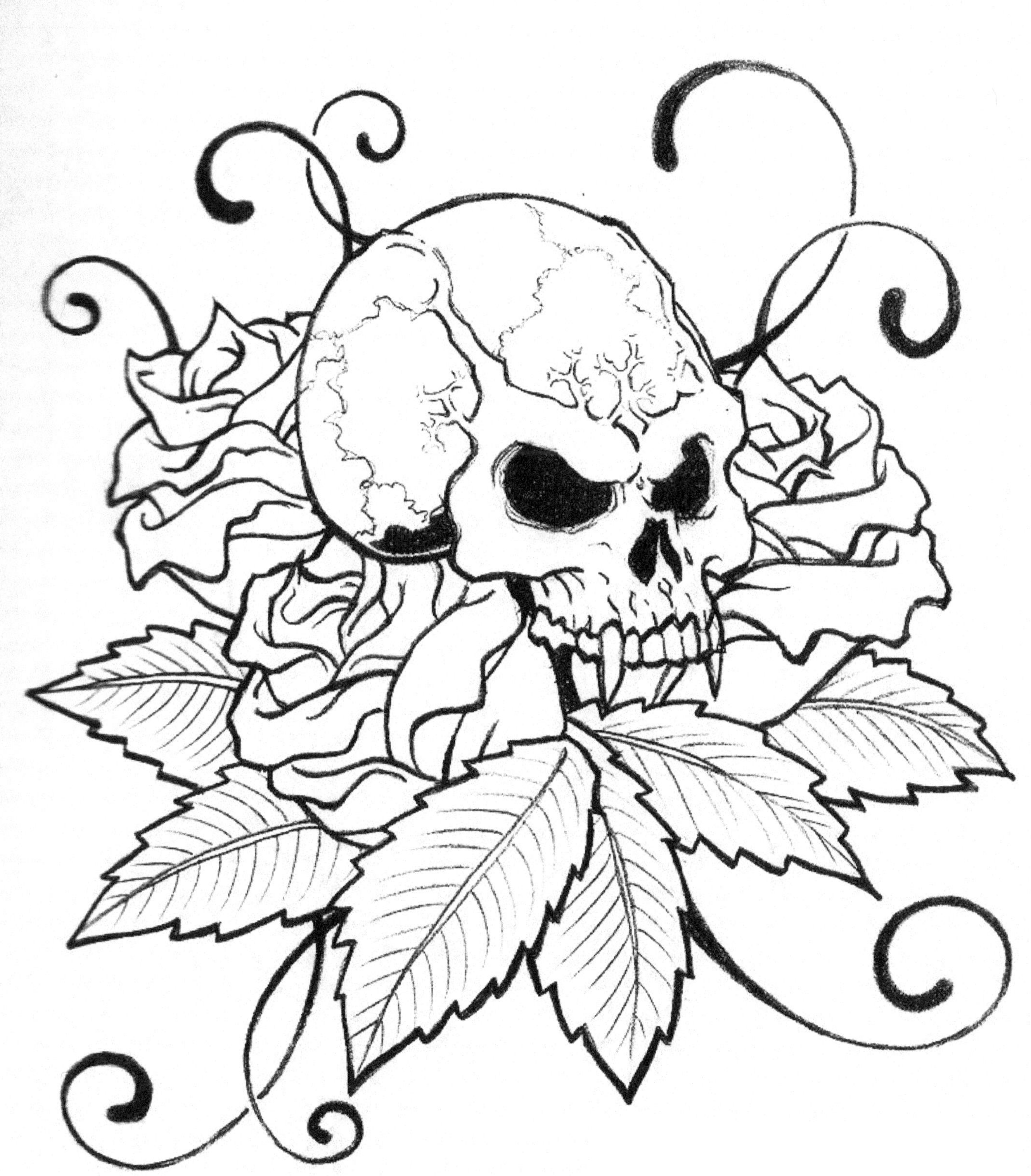

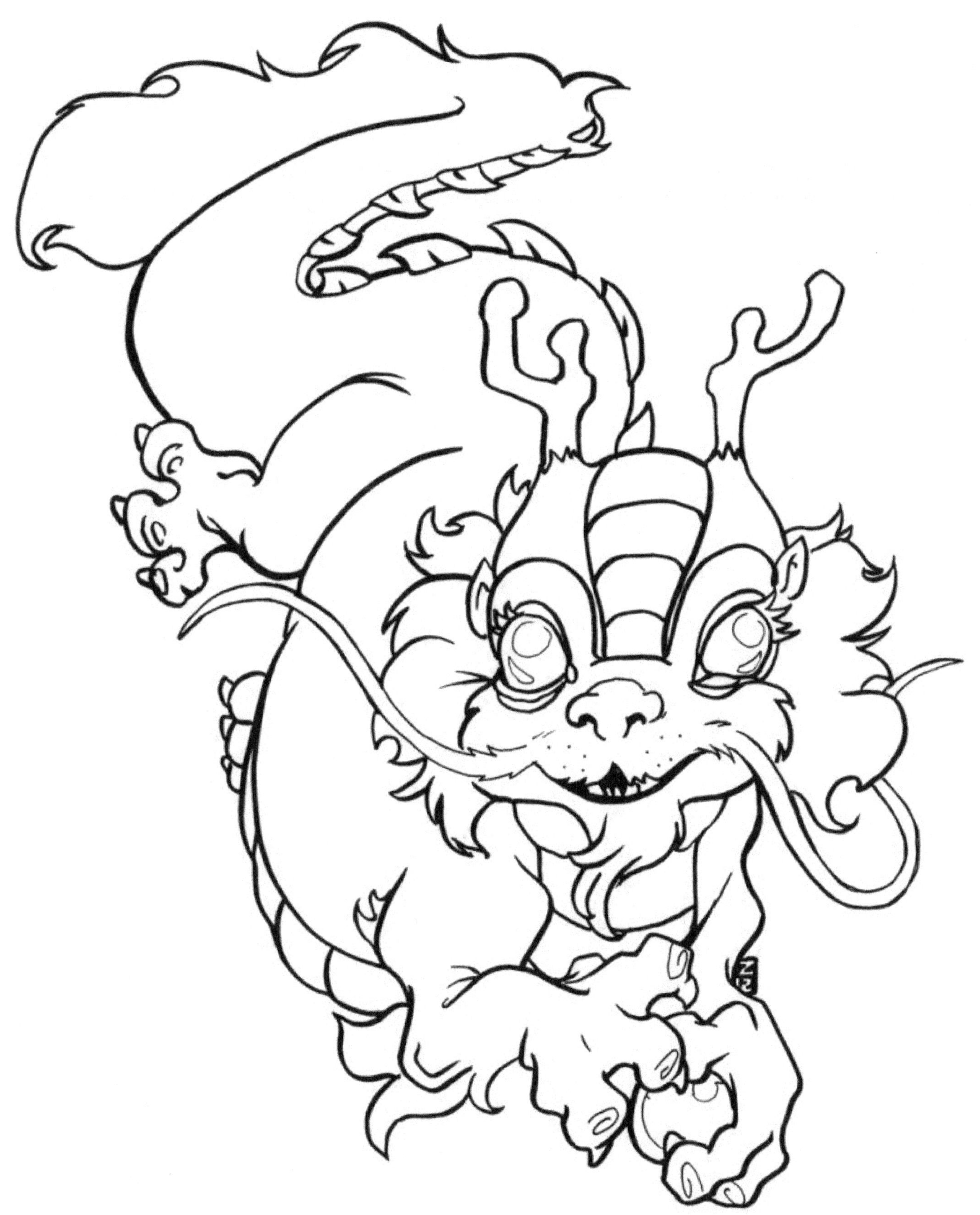

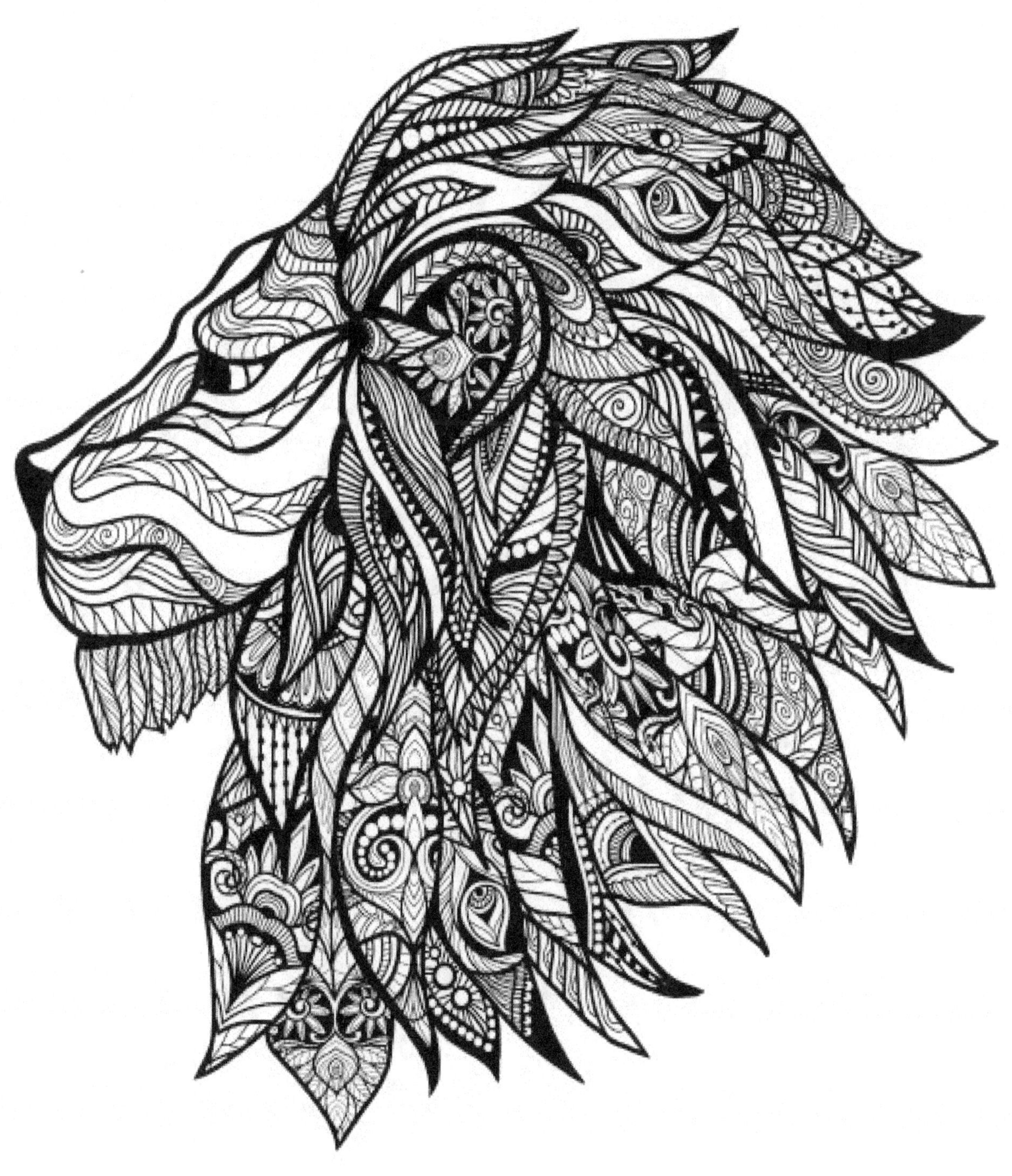

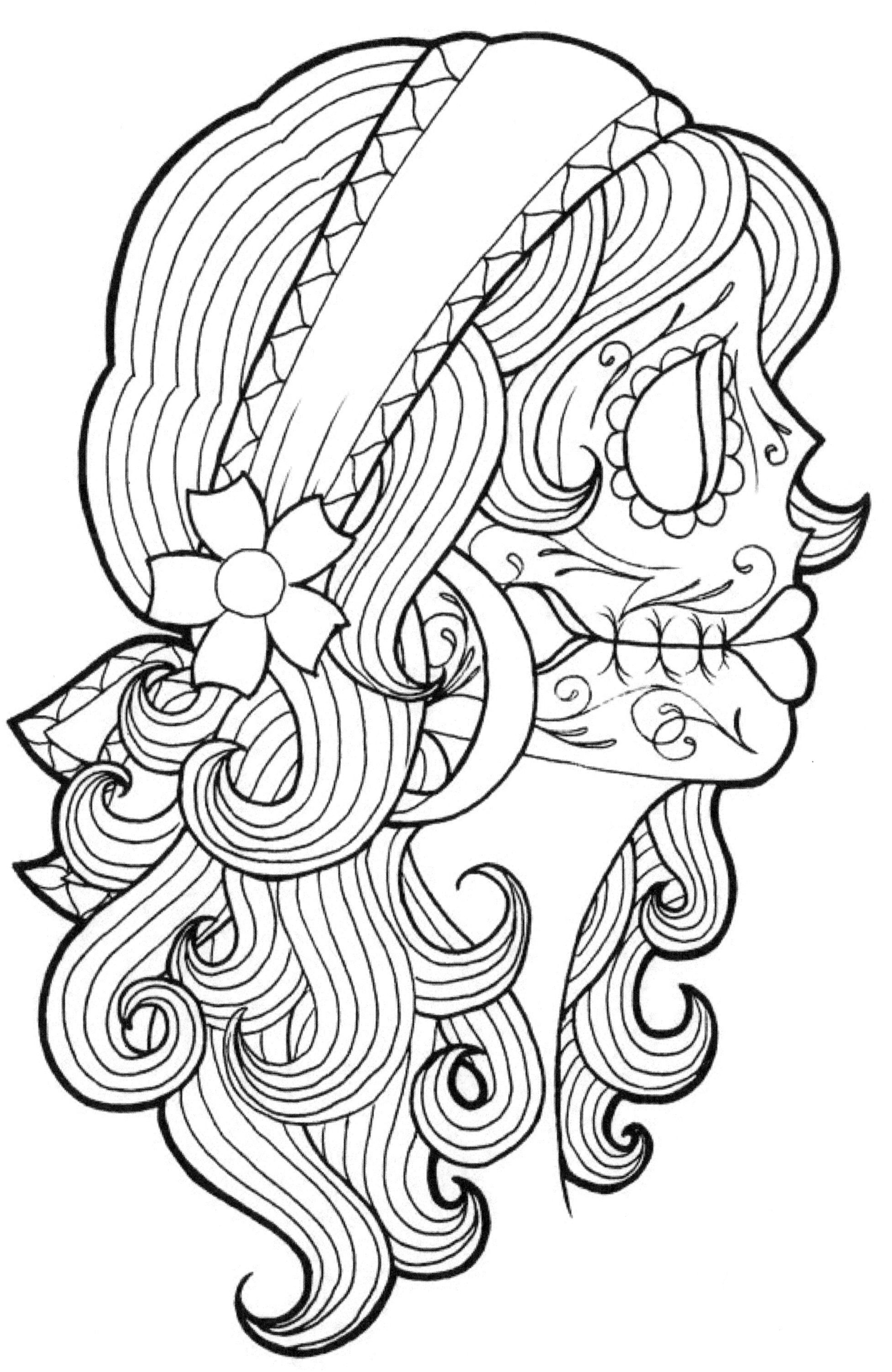

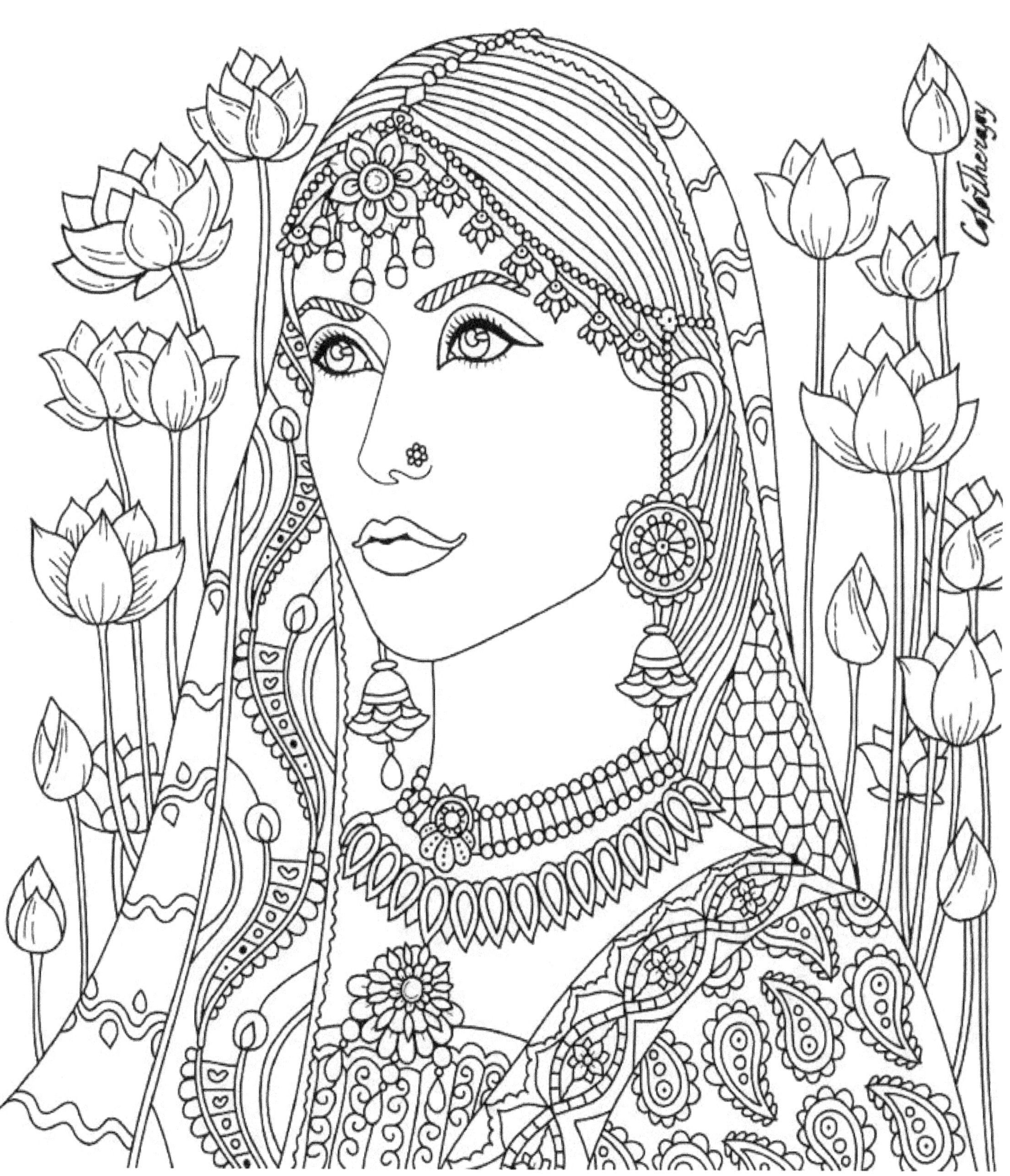
ColorTherapy

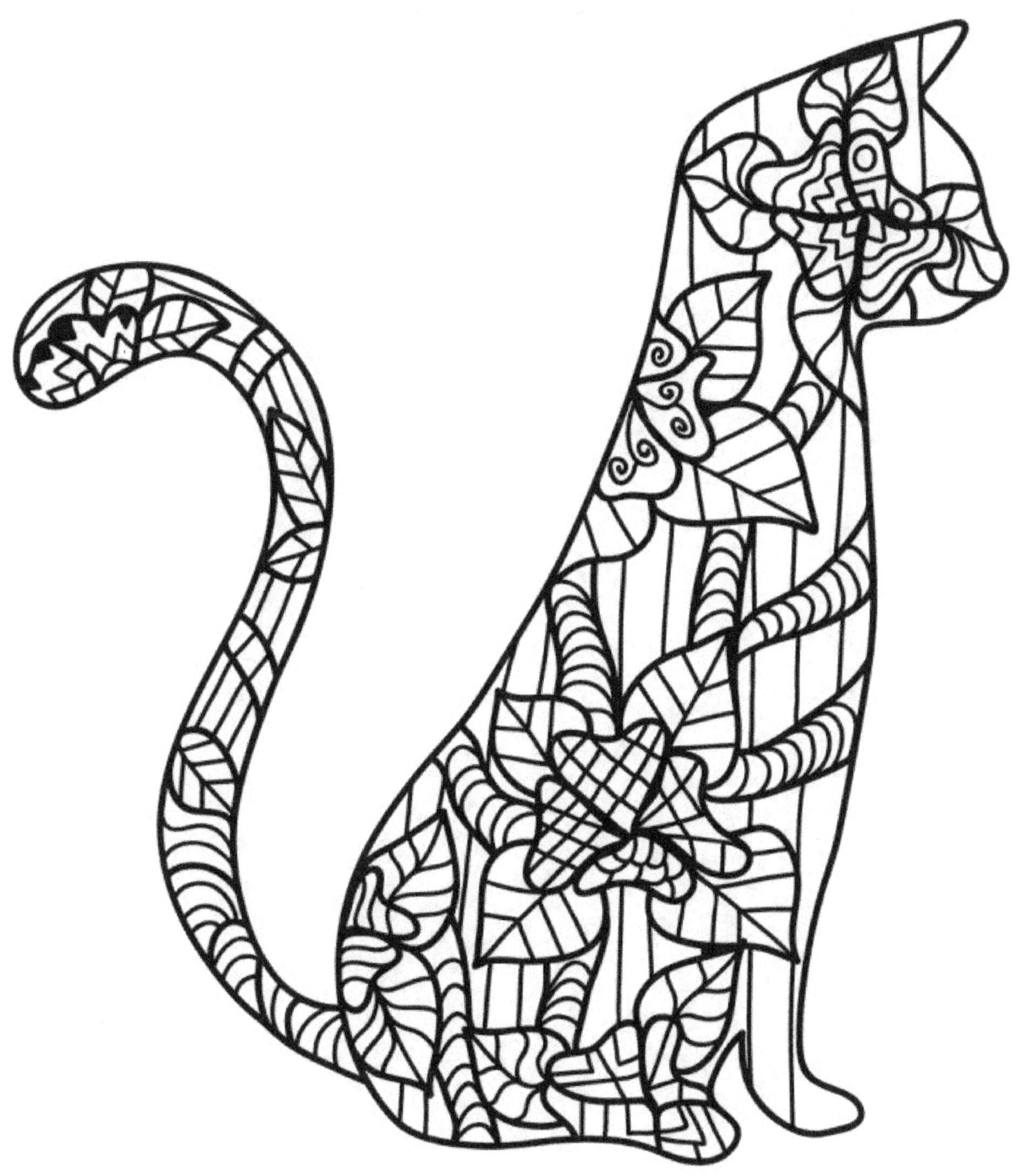

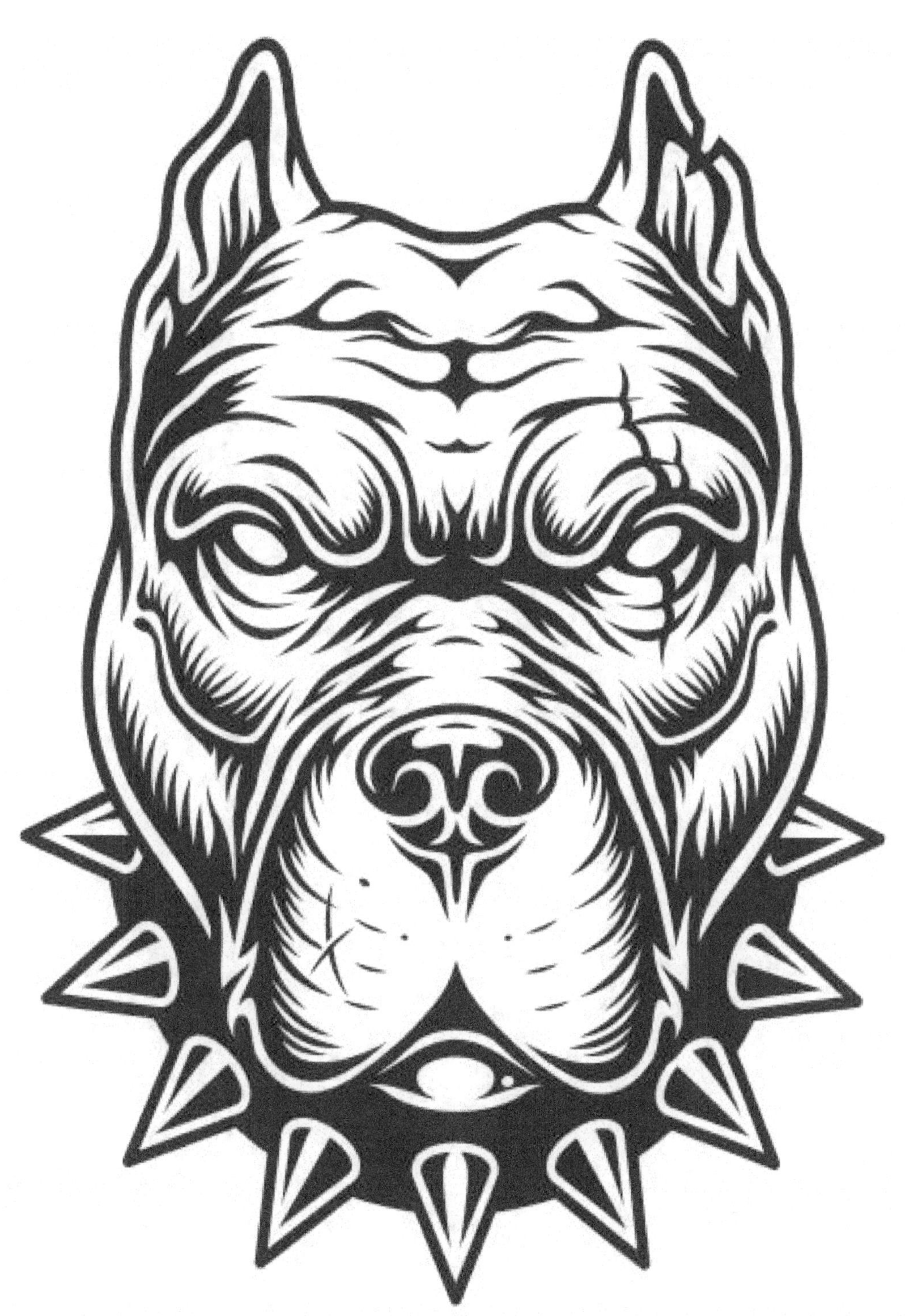

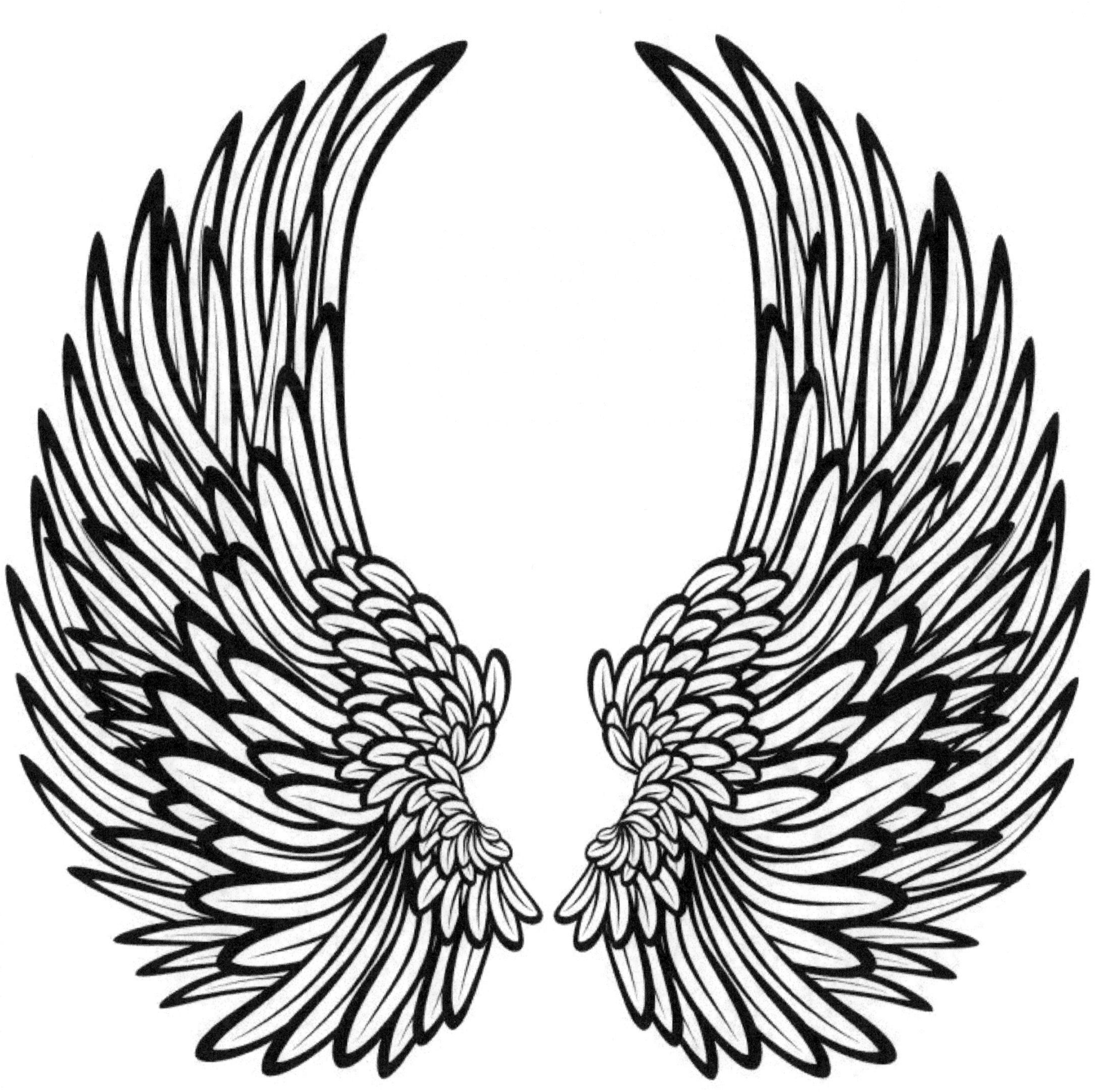

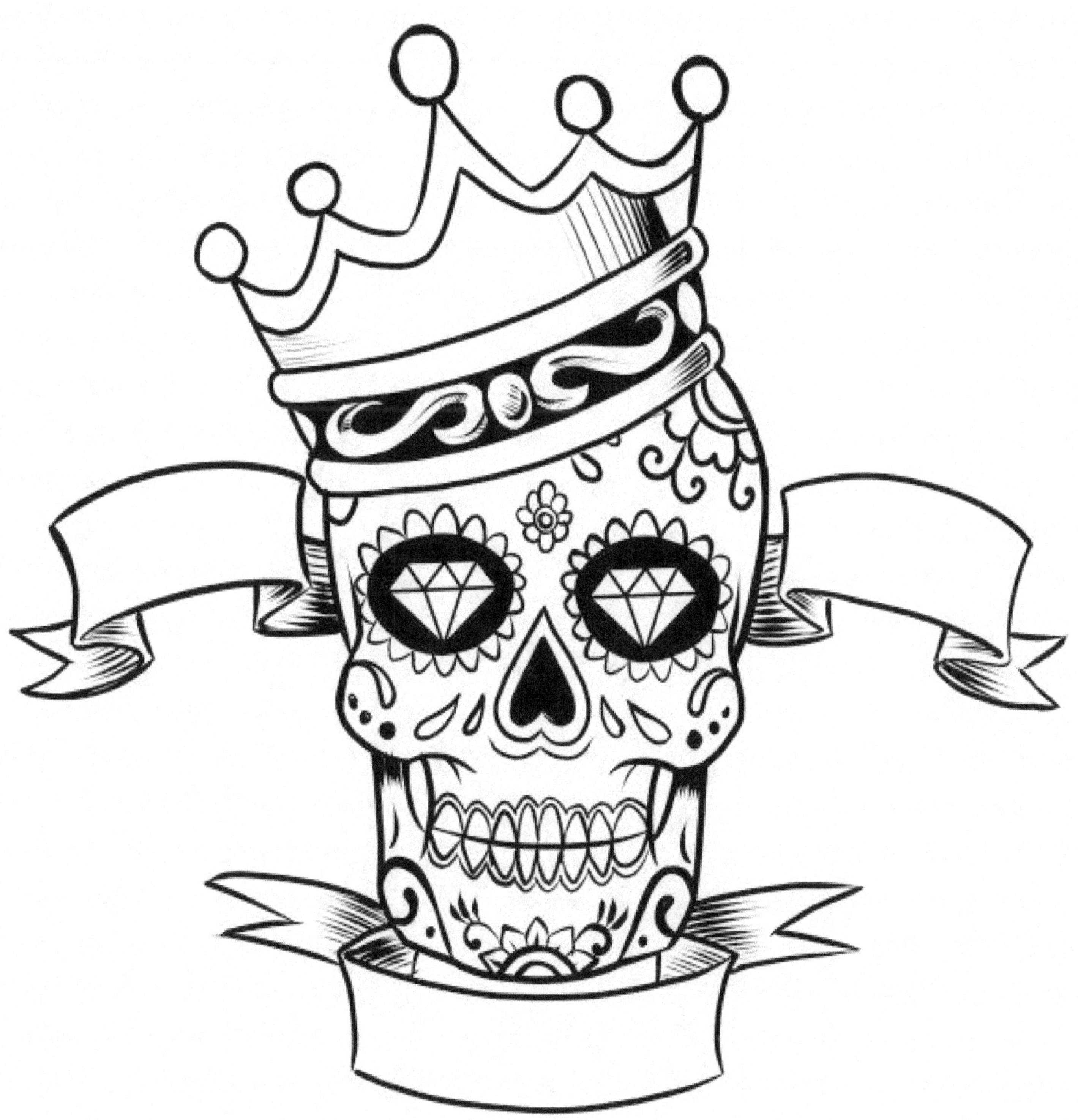

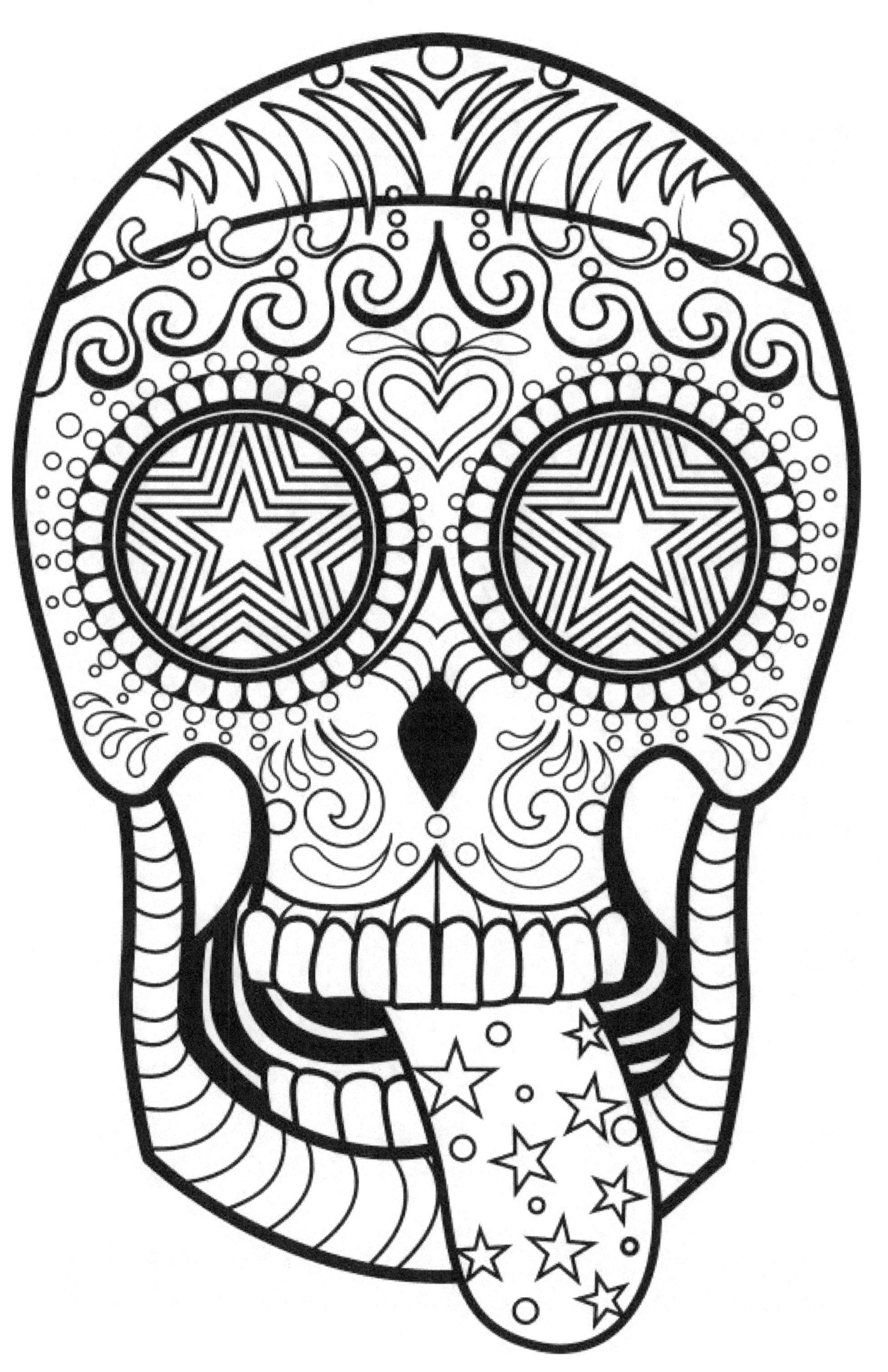

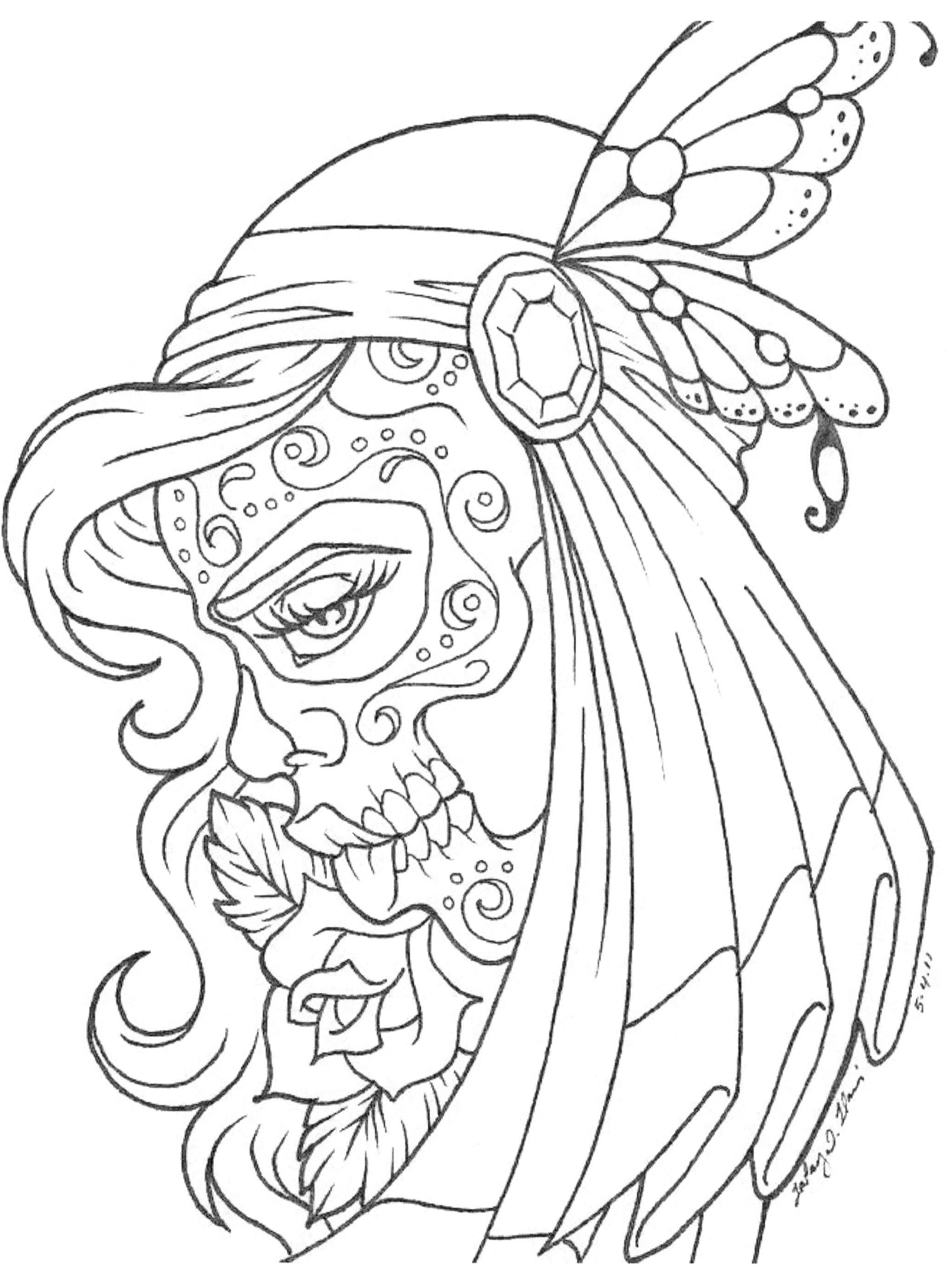

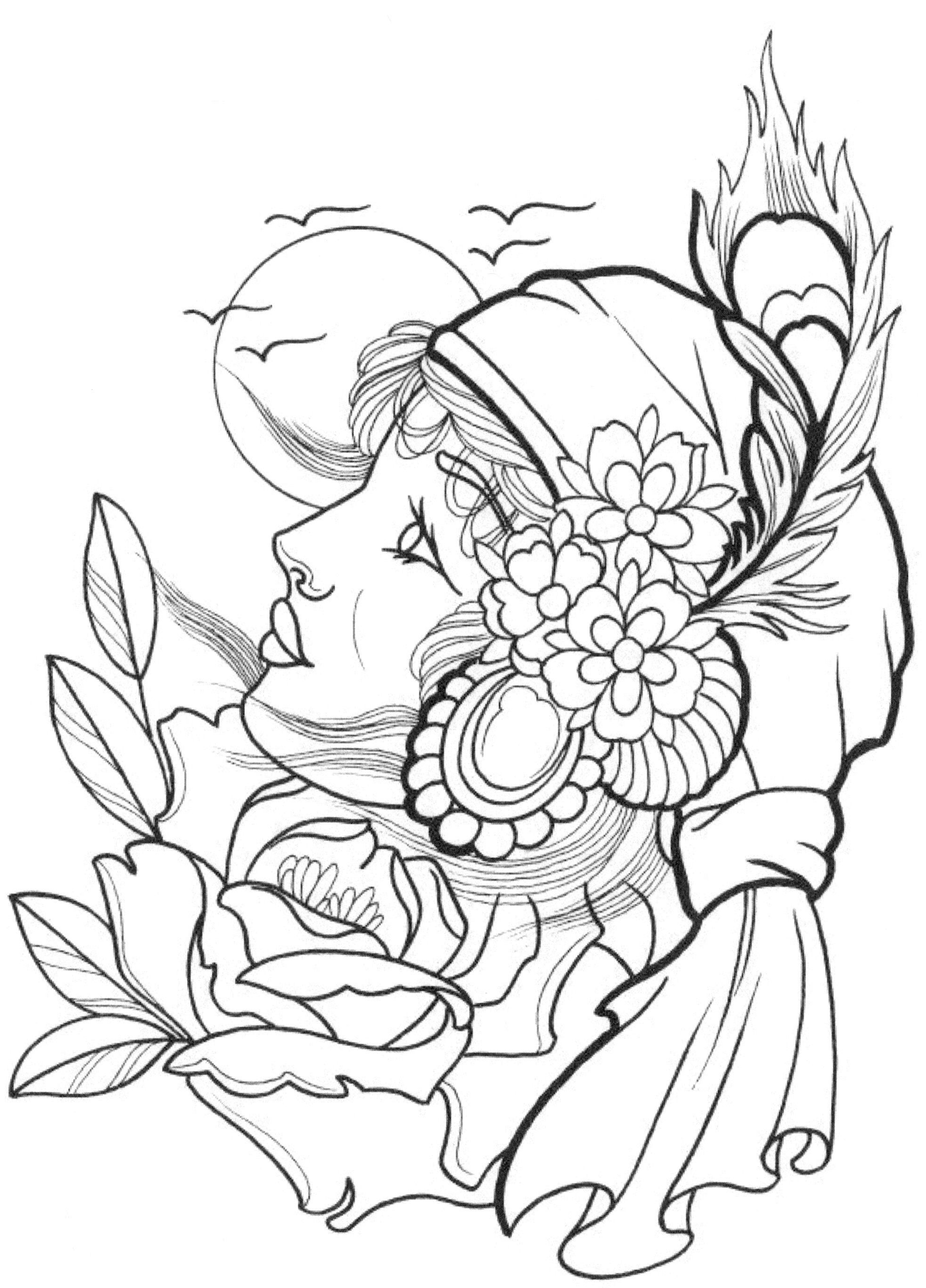

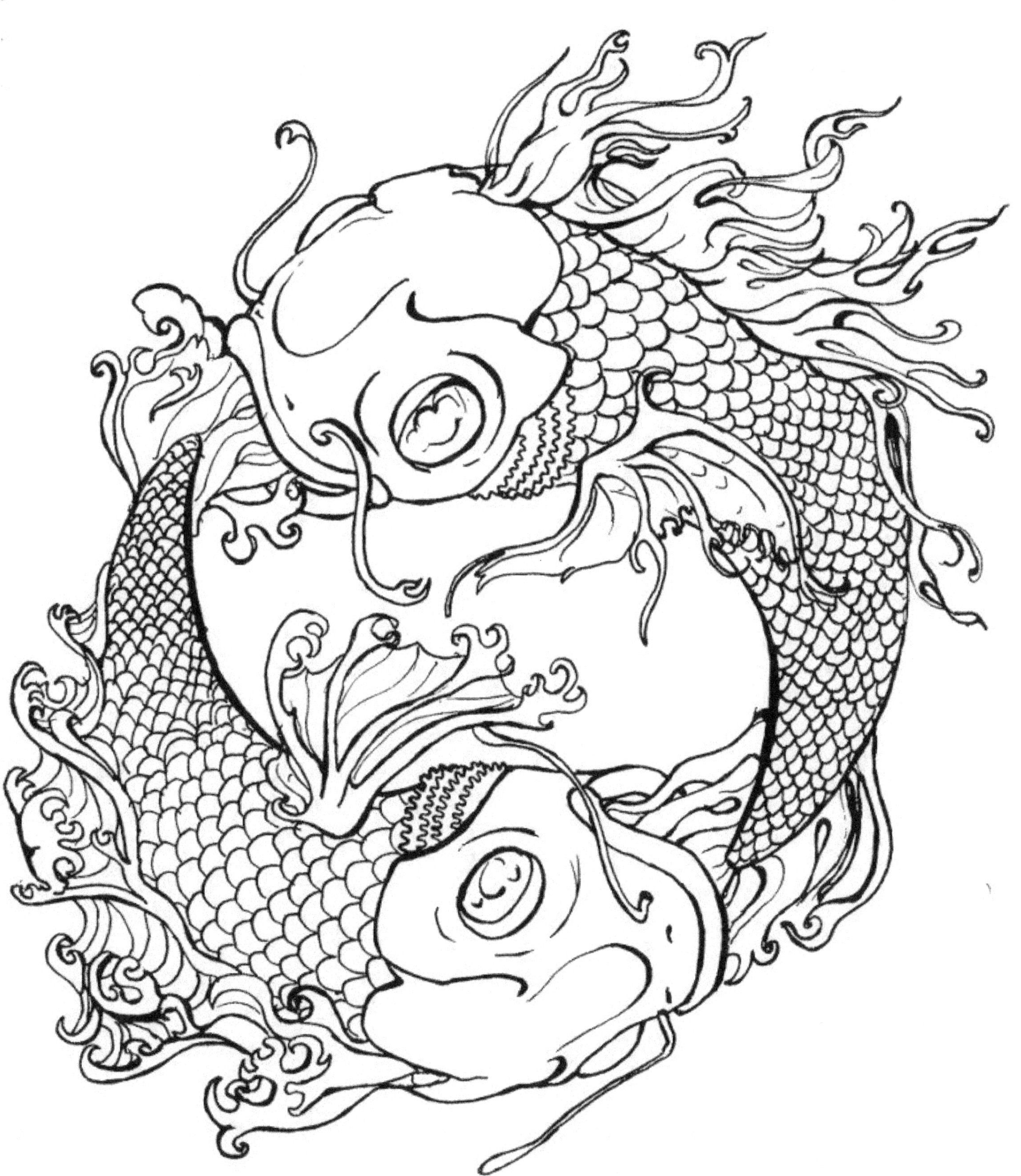